**New Directions for
Student Leadership**

Susan R. Komives
EDITOR-IN-CHIEF

Kathy L. Guthrie
ASSOCIATE EDITOR

M000302316

Going Digital
in Student
Leadership

Josie Ahlquist
Lisa Endersby

Number 153 • Spring 2017
Jossey-Bass
San Francisco

Going Digital in Student Leadership
Josie Ahlquist and Lisa Endersby (eds.)
New Directions for Student Leadership, No. 153, Spring 2017

Editor-in-Chief: *Susan R. Komives*
Associate Editor: *Kathy L. Guthrie*

NEW DIRECTIONS FOR STUDENT LEADERSHIP, (Print ISSN: 2373-3349; Online ISSN: 2373-3357), is published quarterly by Wiley Subscription Services, Inc., a Wiley Company, 111 River St., Hoboken, NJ 07030-5774 USA.
Postmaster: Send all address changes to NEW DIRECTIONS FOR STUDENT LEADERSHIP, John Wiley & Sons Inc., C/O The Sheridan Press, PO Box 465, Hanover, PA 17331 USA.

Information for subscribers
New Directions for Student Leadership is published in 4 issues per year. Institutional subscription prices for 2017 are:
Print & Online: US$462 (US), US$516 (Canada & Mexico), US$562 (Rest of World), €366 (Europe), £290 (UK). Prices are exclusive of tax. Asia-Pacific GST, Canadian GST/HST and European VAT will be applied at the appropriate rates. For more information on current tax rates, please go to www.wileyonlinelibrary.com/tax-vat. The price includes online access to the current and all online backfiles to January 1st 2013, where available. For other pricing options, including access information and terms and conditions, please visit www.wileyonlinelibrary.com/access.

Delivery Terms and Legal Title
Where the subscription price includes print issues and delivery is to the recipient's address, delivery terms are **Delivered at Place (DAP)**; the recipient is responsible for paying any import duty or taxes. Title to all issues transfers FOB our shipping point, freight prepaid. We will endeavour to fulfil claims for missing or damaged copies within six months of publication, within our reasonable discretion and subject to availability.

Back issues: Single issues from current and recent volumes are available at the current single issue price from cs-journals@wiley.com.

Disclaimer
The Publisher and Editors cannot be held responsible for errors or any consequences arising from the use of information contained in this journal; the views and opinions expressed do not necessarily reflect those of the Publisher and Editors, neither does the publication of advertisements constitute any endorsement by the Publisher and Editors of the products advertised.

Publisher: New Directions for Student Leadership is published by Wiley Periodicals, Inc., 350 Main St., Malden, MA 02148-5020.

Journal Customer Services: For ordering information, claims and any enquiry concerning your journal subscription please go to www.wileycustomerhelp.com/ask or contact your nearest office.
Americas: Email: cs-journals@wiley.com; Tel: +1 781 388 8598 or +1 800 835 6770 (toll free in the USA & Canada).
Europe, Middle East and Africa: Email: cs-journals@wiley.com; Tel: +44 (0) 1865 778315.
Asia Pacific: Email: cs-journals@wiley.com; Tel: +65 6511 8000.
Japan: For Japanese speaking support, Email: cs-japan@wiley.com.
Visit our Online Customer Help available in 7 languages at www.wileycustomerhelp.com/ask

Production Editor: Meghanjali Singh (email: mesingh@wiley.com).

Wiley's Corporate Citizenship initiative seeks to address the environmental, social, economic, and ethical challenges faced in our business and which are important to our diverse stakeholder groups. Since launching the initiative, we have focused on sharing our content with those in need, enhancing community philanthropy, reducing our carbon impact, creating global guidelines and best practices for paper use, establishing a vendor code of ethics, and engaging our colleagues and other stakeholders in our efforts. Follow our progress at www.wiley.com/go/citizenship

View this journal online at wileyonlinelibrary.com/journal/yd

Wiley is a founding member of the UN-backed HINARI, AGORA, and OARE initiatives. They are now collectively known as Research4Life, making online scientific content available free or at nominal cost to researchers in developing countries. Please visit Wiley's Content Access – Corporate Citizenship site: http://www.wiley.com/WileyCDA/Section/id-390082.html

Address for Editorial Correspondence: Associate Editor, Kathy L. Guthrie, *New Directions for Student Leadership*, Email: kguthrie@fsu.edu.

Abstracting and Indexing Services
The Journal is indexed by Academic Search (EBSCO Publishing); Academic Search Alumni Edition (EBSCO Publishing); Academic Search Premier (EBSCO Publishing); Environmental Sciences & Pollution Management (ProQuest); ERA: Educational Research Abstracts Online (T&F); ERIC: Educational Resources Information Center (CSC); Health & Safety Science Abstracts (ProQuest); MEDLINE/PubMed (NLM); Pollution Abstracts (ProQuest); Professional Development Collection (EBSCO Publishing); PsycINFO/Psychological Abstracts (APA); Safety Science & Risk Abstracts (ProQuest); SocINDEX (EBSCO Publishing); Studies on Women & Gender Abstracts (T&F).

Cover design: Wiley
Cover Images: © Lava 4 images | Shutterstock

For submission instructions, subscription and all other information visit:
wileyonlinelibrary.com/journal/yd

Contents

EDITORS' NOTES   5
Josie Ahlquist, Lisa Endersby

1. Remixing Leadership Practices with Emerging Technologies   9
Edmund T. Cabellon, Paul Gordon Brown
The authors present an overview of the historical trends in and current
state of technology in education (P–20), including platforms, tools, and
theories that have influenced this area.

2. Leadership 2.0: The Impact of Technology on Leadership   21
Development
John L. Hoffman, Cara Vorhies
Technological innovation has become a driver of educational and leadership development practices that place students at the center of learning and leadership development experiences. Recommendations for
equitable and inclusive practice in using technology in leadership development are discussed.

3. P–20 Model of Digital Citizenship   35
Marialice B. F. X. Curran, Mike Ribble
This chapter explores a P–20 digital citizenship model that builds upon
the respect, educate, and protect model beginning with our earliest
learners through elementary, middle, high school, and college.

4. Digital Student Leadership Development   47
Josie Ahlquist
Social media tools are ubiquitous throughout the college student experience, particularly for students who hold leadership positions on
campus. A research study on junior and senior student leaders' social
media use and experience led to a number of findings that inform leadership education practice.

5. Student Activism in the Technology Age   63
Adam Gismondi, Laura Osteen
This chapter discusses the emergent use of digital technology to inspire,
connect, and sustain student activism on campus. An overview of student activism, opportunities, and challenges of this technology, along
with recent case studies and implications for practice, are presented.

6. The Virtual Table: A Framework for Online Teamwork,   75
Collaboration, and Communication
Lisa Endersby, Kirstin Phelps, Dan Jenkins
This chapter reviews the complex relationship between technology and
leadership, focusing on how technology affects the development and
demonstration of skills in communication, teamwork, and collaboration. The chapter also proposes a framework for identifying and assessing key leadership competencies in the digital space.

7. A Mindset for Career Curiosity: Emerging Leaders Working   89
in the Digital Space
Mallory Bower, Peter Konwerski
This chapter addresses the rapid growth of American industry, and a
proposed framework—the mindset for career curiosity—that can be
used to prepare students for quickly evolving 21st-century digital work
environments.

INDEX   103

Editors' Notes

Never before has there been such a dramatic shift in how educators recruit, teach, assess, and support students as future leaders. The anticipated and measured changes in student demographics and diversity of educational options have been greatly affected by the advent of digital technologies. From learning management systems to the implementation of online teaching tools, institutions have seen a collective shift both in how high school and college students learn and how practitioners work to provide meaningful learning experiences. This volume of *New Directions for Student Leadership* broadens the scholarly research and pedagogical discussions of technology beyond student leadership development to include unique opportunities and challenges for leadership education in this new digital age. No text yet has considered these complex intersections of theory, practice, and pedagogy with technology and student leadership development.

Technology in this volume is broadly defined beyond more traditionally identified media such as Facebook, Twitter, and Snapchat. Whereas social media represents a key and timely influence on leadership education, technology also encompasses digital learning tools and platforms in which students, faculty, and administrators can share and critically examine leadership theories and identities. Technology, then, is a tool by which educators can influence and educate youth across all stages of leadership development. Leadership itself can now look different in online spaces and students must find new ways to develop and demonstrate essential skills in teamwork, communication, and conflict management. This volume examines the impact of technology on both the scholarship and practice of leadership education.

Like all texts discussing technology, it is a constant challenge to keep pace with the continual evolution of advances in the field. By the time this volume is published, there will be multiple new studies, findings, and tools that will only further enhance and complicate our understanding of student leadership development in these online spaces. In an effort to keep pace with this change, a variety of sources were drawn upon including published journals, dissertation research, and recent news stories. The authors and editors also made an intentional effort to include content that spans middle school to postsecondary graduation, building, for example, from the digital competencies and skills from the International Society for Technology in Education (ISTE, 2007), digital citizenship in K–12 (Ribble, 2015) and the infusion of digital leadership in higher education (Ahlquist, 2015). Another core of the volume integrates the professional competency areas for student affairs educators by ACPA: College Student Educators International and NASPA: Student Affairs Professionals in Higher Education. The new technology competency is defined as follows:

> Focuses on the use of digital tools, resources, and technologies for the advancement of student learning, development, and success as well as the improved performance of student affairs professionals. Included within this area are knowledge, skills, and dispositions that lead to the generation of digital literacy and digital citizenship within communities of students, student affairs professionals, faculty members, and colleges and universities as a whole. (ACPA/NASPA, 2015, p. 15)

This competency reminds us that technology is no longer an optional inclusion in our practice. The attitude of not being "into" technology can no longer be an excuse for not exploring the innovative possibilities of including digital tools in leadership education. The goal of this volume is to encourage a technology-open mindset in educators committed to providing timely, meaningful, and accessible learning opportunities. The competency and the articles presented in this volume both offer ways to explore the impact of technology in our field while also proposing ways in which practitioners can integrate technology into their work. Educators must no longer be content with racing to catch up with our students and the changing digital landscape; we must now learn to keep pace.

This volume aims to critically examine and discuss how technology has affected, does affect, and will affect our work in preparing students to be future leaders, workers, and learners. We have aimed to provide a comprehensive perspective on leadership education in the digital age, including discussions on working, learning, and leading in these online spaces. Chapter authors have integrated a dual focus on understanding how educators can best prepare students for this new age of education while also developing in this space ourselves, no matter whether our work is in elementary, secondary, or postsecondary education.

To this end, chapters in this volume cover both the scholarship of leadership theory and the practice of leadership education as they intersect with emerging technological tools and platforms. Early chapters offer insight into how technology has affected understandings of leadership in a higher education context, conceptualizing traditional theories and examining how both students and administrators navigate this new, complex landscape. The volume continues with discussions of important considerations for our work with students as developing leaders, highlighting topics of digital citizenship, social media use, and activism that combine leadership education with technology as a tool and a tactic. The current educational context and global environment in which leadership is practiced demands a critical lens for reviewing leadership curriculum and pedagogy, particularly in how technology has shaped the identification and development of leaders at all levels. The volume concludes with discussions of how leadership development on campus translates to effective leadership off campus, where digital tools will continue to play a vital role in a student's personal and professional growth.

Our call to colleagues after reading this volume is one of optimism and encouragement. Going digital in student leadership will guide educators, remix theory, and inspire technology practices to meet the unique digital experiences and needs of today's students. Although there will always be challenges in this space of expanded access to information and individuals, the opportunity for increased connection and enhanced pedagogical practice can only benefit students, educators, and ourselves as we enter an exciting new frontier of leadership education and practice. We are truly grateful to our colleagues who have contributed to this volume and hope those who read it will be inspired to integrate digital and social technologies into their leadership development practice.

Josie Ahlquist
Lisa Endersby
Editors

References

ACPA: College Student Educators International, & NASPA: Student Affairs Administrators in Higher Education. (2015). *ACPA/NASPA professional competency areas for student affairs practitioners* (2nd ed.). Washington, DC: Authors.

Ahlquist, J. (2015). Developing digital student leaders: A mixed methods study of student leadership, identity, and decision making on social media (Doctoral dissertation). Retrieved from ProQuest Dissertations and Theses. (Accession Order No. 3713711)

International Society for Technology in Education. (2007). *ISTE standards for students.* Retrieved from http://www.iste.org/standards/iste-standards/standards-for-students

Ribble, M. (2015). *Digital citizenship in schools* (3rd ed.). Eugene, OR: International Society for Technology in Education.

JOSIE AHLQUIST is a research associate and instructor in the Florida State University Leadership Learning Research Center, teaching undergraduate and master's courses based in technology and leadership. She is also an independent leadership speaker, educating students, higher education administrators, and faculty around the globe on digital leadership curriculum. For the third year in a row, she has been named to the "Top 50 Must Read Higher Education Technology Blogs" by Ed Tech Magazine, blogging at www.josieahlquist.com.

LISA ENDERSBY is a doctoral student exploring professional development in online communities of practice at the University of Windsor. She is past national chair of the NASPA Technology Knowledge Community. Among her numerous publications and presentations is a recent chapter in Leadership 2050: Critical Challenges, Key Contexts, and Emerging Trends, by the International Leadership Association (ILA). Lisa is also coeditor of "Pause for Pedagogy," a monthly article series in the ILA newsletter exploring innovative pedagogical practices and strategies in leadership education.

NEW DIRECTIONS FOR STUDENT LEADERSHIP • DOI: 10.1002/yd

1

The authors present an overview of the historical trends in and current state of technology in leadership education (P–20), including the influence of related platforms, tools, and theories.

Remixing Leadership Practices with Emerging Technologies

Edmund T. Cabellon, Paul Gordon Brown

With the introduction of digital and social technologies, information and ideas are now more easily shared and spread than ever before. With the click of a mouse or the touch of a screen, individuals can connect with others, organize for change, and spread their ideas and information with relative ease. Given these new affordances and abilities provided by technology, the landscape for leadership is changing and the world needs leaders who are conversant in and can adapt quickly to technological change. Leadership and related educational programs have an important role to play in developing the next generation of digital leaders, but these programs can be effective only if the educators themselves understand the complexities of leadership in a digital age.

Educators are increasingly recognizing the importance of digital tools and spaces in accomplishing the goals of leadership education programs designed for students. For example, some programs include the use of multimedia content, electronic portfolios, mobile websites, and applications (Dalton, 2007). Additionally, other leadership programs use social networking sites to engage students in ongoing conversations or prompted discussions (Ahlquist, 2015). The deployment and use of digital tools in leadership has grown over the past decade. Educators are also increasingly taking a more positive stance toward technological integration, framing technology in a more balanced way by recognizing technology's challenges and benefits (Lederman & Jaschik, 2013). Although these shifts are positive, further work can be done to ensure current and subsequent generations of leaders are competent in the use of digital and social technology tools.

Leadership education requires a new set of knowledge, competencies, and skills in light of societal changes brought on by technology. It is a fallacy to assume that just because young leaders have grown up using digital

NEW DIRECTIONS FOR STUDENT LEADERSHIP, no. 153, Spring 2017 © 2017 Wiley Periodicals, Inc., A Wiley Company
Published online in Wiley Online Library (wileyonlinelibrary.com) • DOI: 10.1002/yd.20226

and social technologies that they are necessarily savvy in its use toward goal-driven ends (Harvard Business Review, 2010; Spitzer, Morel, Buvat, & Subrahmanyam, 2013). All students, and emerging adults in particular, require a new set of competencies and skills in order to be effective leaders (International Society for Technology in Education [ISTE], 2007). Additionally, educators must also develop skills in order to engage with students and develop programs that are relevant in today's increasingly digital contexts (ACPA: College Student Educators International & NASPA: Student Affairs Administrators in Higher Education, 2015; ISTE, 2007).

This chapter makes the case that the use of digital and social technology in education is no longer optional, but necessary in order to develop effective leaders. This chapter provides an overview of technology's influence on students and educators; important knowledge, skills, and competencies needed by both groups; and specific tools and suggestions for their deployment in educational environments. The chapter concludes with recommendations on how to be an effective leadership educator in light of current technology trends.

The Impact of Technology on Leadership Education

Throughout this volume, the authors discuss the various impacts of digital and social technology on students, educators, and educational practice as it relates to leadership. To set the stage for this discussion it is important to understand the complexities of how technology affects these groups. Youth are confronting issues related to an altered learning and developmental environment, issues of reputation management and identity, and how to be effective digital citizens. Educators are confronting shifts in pedagogical approaches, issues of technology accessibility, and a need for additional training and professional development.

Technology's Influence on the Student Experience. As a result of technology's pervading influence in contemporary life, today's students must navigate a significantly expanded and different world than their predecessors did. Educators looking for research on how technology affects the developmental and learning experiences of student leaders will find a literature that is relatively new and evolving. A number of researchers, however, are beginning to examine these areas—including issues of digital identity, reputation, and civic engagement (Ahlquist, 2015; Brown, 2016; Eaton, 2015; Gismondi, 2015). In addition to learning and development, technology is revolutionizing the tools that student leaders use to organize, communicate, and establish and maintain relationships (Gismondi, 2015). Much of this technological change centers around social media and related social technologies. Given the intimacy of social technologies and the human experience, educators should be cognizant that an altered learning environment may affect issues of student learning, development, and identity construction—a topic discussed further in Chapter 4.

NEW DIRECTIONS FOR STUDENT LEADERSHIP • DOI: 10.1002/yd

Contemporary student leaders are confronted with more complex issues of reputation and impression management than their predecessors (Ahlquist, 2015; Brown, 2016; Qualman, 2015). Social media, in particular, play a significant role in raising the public profile of all students in a way that extends beyond the physical boundaries of a traditional campus. Although students in formal leadership positions have always experienced being watched more closely than their peers, social and digital media amplify the effect (Qualman, 2015). When a student leader makes a mistake online, it can quickly spread across campus in a matter of minutes and potentially be picked up by local, national, and international news outlets. Quick searches for college students behaving badly online will result in stories of students who were fired from internships, fraternities that were suspended, and student athletes who had draft potentials revoked (Qualman, 2015). As a result of this change, student leaders need to be more cognizant than ever about their reputation and how their actions reflect on the groups of which they are a part (Qualman, 2015).

Contemporary students are also confronted with a world in which civic engagement and social action are intertwined with digital environments. Education for "digital citizenship" is increasingly important in order to best prepare students for engagement in civil society. Digital citizenship calls for students to "understand human, cultural, and societal issues related to technology and practice legal and ethical behavior" (ISTE, 2007, p. 2). Digital citizenship goes beyond the mere understanding and use of digital tools and highlights the importance of teaching leadership behaviors within the contexts created by these tools. Digital citizenship education can include skills such as how to interact civilly online by posting and responding to feedback appropriately and how to responsibly share and consume more reliable news and information sources. These competencies are addressed later in this chapter and in detail in Chapter 3.

Technology's Influence on the Educator Experience.   Alongside students, educators confront a unique set of challenges and issues related to the increasing prevalence and centrality of technology in society. Technology's influence requires a shift in pedagogical approaches—both inside and outside of the classroom. Within the classroom, higher education faculty have experimented with "flipped classrooms" by asking students to watch prerecorded lectures and review presentation slides before class, in order to devote in-classroom time to group project work, discussion, and knowledge application (Kim, Kim, Khera, & Getman, 2014). Increasingly, students take courses that are entirely online or in hybrid formats blending online coursework with physical classroom seat time (Bowen, 2013). As a result of these changes, some institutions have initiated mandatory laptop purchase programs for their students to ensure all of those who are enrolled have the necessary devices and software to fully participate (Kay & Lauricella, 2011). Intentional participation in online and hybrid courses has generally shown a positive relationship between the use of these technologies and student engagement (Chen, Lambert, & Guidry, 2010).

Within the high school context, teachers have used social media tools, such as Twitter, to extend classroom discussions outside of the bounds of classroom seat time (McWilliams, Hickey, Hines, Conner, & Bishop, 2011). The use of technology extends to elementary schools where teachers have added the use of tablets to keep their students engaged through electronic activities augmenting the formal curriculum (Ditzler, Hong, & Strudler, 2016). Technology is affecting and shifting pedagogical practice across all educational levels, yet traditional paradigms remain dominant (Bowen, 2013).

Although technology use and experimentation is on the rise, access to technology remains a crosscurrent and barrier to its integration into educational environments. In elementary and high schools, limited funding can prevent administrators from building a technology infrastructure—including WiFi access points, computer labs, and software (Hassan & Geys, 2016). Within higher education, there are often more resources dedicated to technological infrastructure, but commuter and adult populations may be constrained by a lack of Internet access at home—a challenge to educators using learning management systems and other technologies (Brown, Wohn, & Ellison, 2016). Device access compounds these issues. Because educators teach students from a variety of socioeconomic backgrounds, many of these students may have varying access to tablets and computers (Bowen, 2013). This "have and have not" paradigm creates inconsistencies when developing opportunities for formal education across digital platforms.

Finally, educators across all educational levels lack the professional development necessary to keep up with demands for digital technology integration. Even if a college or school has the resources to purchase software, they may nevertheless lack the proper staffing and infrastructure to fully implement and support the software (Roberts-Mahoney, Means, & Garrison, 2016). Additionally, as educators comply with federal and state mandates on standards and testing, teachers must devote preparation time and adopt pedagogies to "teach to the test" rather than experiment with the use of digital technology. In order to be effective teachers using digital tools, a more integrative approach to incorporating digital tools topics is necessary.

Technology Knowledge, Skills, and Competencies for Student Leaders and Educators

A number of organizations have begun to codify the knowledge, skills, and competencies that educators and students need in order to be successful in the digital age. These standards and competencies form the basis for the integration of technology into the curriculum and cocurriculum and act as guidelines for educators seeking to remain current. For example, in 2007, ISTE developed a set of standards for teaching and learning in the digital age—providing an important baseline for leadership education incorporating digital issues and tools into the K–12 environment. The ISTE (2007) Standards for Students identify and categorize desirable digital knowledge and skills into six domains: (a) creativity and innovation; (b) communication and collaboration; (c) research and information fluency; (d) critical thinking, problem solving, and decision making; (e) digital citizenship; and (f) technology operations and concepts. These domains highlight the need to understand how to use digital tools, navigate online environments, and use these tools to lead and enact change.

Educators themselves must continue to remain current with technological trends in order to be effective partners in the learning process with students. In 2015, ACPA and NASPA updated their suggested competencies for college student educators to include a stand-alone technology competency, rather than treating technology as a topic threaded throughout all of the competencies. The competencies state that educators must be conversant in a number of areas that relate to both their educative and administrative roles. Themes present in the recommended competencies include (a) general knowledge and skills related to technology, including the tools and their application for learning and development; (b) issues related to technology and data security and inclusion and accessibility; and (c) fluency in digital media literacy, reputation management, and the personal use of technology for professional development. Perhaps most salient and tangible in this list is the need to be conversant in digital tools. The next sections provide an overview of some of the contemporary tools available to educators and the potential uses.

Digital Tools for Student Leaders and Leadership Educators

When used effectively, digital software, tools, and platforms can enhance the education of student leaders as well as the work of student leaders themselves. Within the past decade, technological device ownership has increasingly reached toward a point of near ubiquity. Among college students in the United States, approximately 90% own laptops and an even higher percentage own smartphones (Dahlstrom, Brooks, Grajek, & Reeves, 2015). In particular, it is the rise of mobile technology that is having one of the most profound impacts on educational and leadership practices. In 2015, the number of college students in the United States owning smartphones surpassed that of laptops for the first time (Dahlstrom et al., 2015). As technology and subsequently Internet access and use continue to rise, more educators, staff, and students report using smartphones as their main digital technology tool (Duggan, 2015).

When using these devices, 92% of emerging adults between the ages of 18 and 29 report using them for social media and engaging on social networking sites (Perrin & Duggan, 2015). Social technologies are increasingly important tools in leadership education surfacing issues and opportunities for student leaders and leadership educators alike. For example:

- Social networking sites, such as Facebook, Twitter, and Instagram, allow individuals to construct profiles, build and maintain relationships, share information, and organize for social change (boyd & Ellison, 2007). As emerging leaders explore their identities online at an earlier age, intentional conversations around these topics are increasingly critical. These discussions can provide important opportunities to help students understand their leadership roles and the contexts in which they lead.
- By their very nature, social technologies are collaborative and community-based communication systems that are of vital importance to the way a modern leader engages (Joosten, 2012). For leaders and educators, this requires moving beyond viewing social technology as purely for personal communication and toward its potential as a professional tool—a tool that can help improve efficiency and productivity. To aid student leaders, leadership educators can spearhead efforts to establish and maintain a program or department's social media presence. Furthermore, by participating in these efforts, student leaders can practice and engage in peer learning in a lower stakes environment (Junco, 2014).
- A number of studies have explored issues of student engagement online including in classroom contexts (Heiberger & Harper, 2008), within first-year success programs (Logan, 2015), and in social adjustment to college (Grey, Vitak, Easton, & Ellison, 2013). These studies provide important data to help contextualize how engagement takes place and can guide the incorporation of digital tools into specific educational programs and services. Different contexts require different tools and approaches to their use.
- College-age students produce more Internet content–including written communications, music, and videos—than any other demographic (Junco, 2014). The rise of mobile devices has also encouraged increased content sharing and collection (Cabellon & Junco, 2015). If harnessed intentionally, these advancements allow for reach and collaboration beyond university walls, potentially expanding the learning environment into broader contexts for student knowledge creation and application.
- Although research has documented a number of in-classroom academic uses of technology (Matias & Wolf, 2013), technologies can also be applied in the cocurricular context. For example, a student organization could use mobile document collaboration and sharing technologies to take meeting notes, develop strategic plans, and design programs and events. Fellow organizational members can collaborate in real time, engage in discussion, and establish tasks and

action items without needing to be physically present with one another. Additionally, students can engage each other online through photographs, live video streams, and event recordings shared through social networking sites.

Because of these trends, social and mobile technologies have the potential to become the primary tools for increased student interaction, collaboration, and peer-to-peer learning (Gikas & Grant, 2013). Many students are introduced to technology through their personal use of it, but their professional and educational use of digital technology is becoming increasingly common (Duggan, 2015). Although technology's incorporation into the learning environment is increasingly welcome, students may experience dissonance as faculty members explore, experiment, make mistakes, and find success with technology in the classroom (Dunlap & Lowenthal, 2009). When it comes to technology, students and educators often find themselves on equal footing—learning and making mistakes together.

Underlying the specific applications of these tools are the shifting ways in which technology is changing and challenging educational paradigms. Successful educational leaders view technology-enhanced learning environments as global communities in which access to learning is not restricted by externally imposed space and time constraints, but rather where flexible learning is valued and practiced by both educators and students (Wankel & Blessinger, 2013). Additionally, successful educational leaders recognize that anytime and anywhere learning environments foster a greater sense of immediacy, interactivity, and authenticity, furthering educational outcomes. In this way, technology may serve as an educational gateway to broader learning opportunities that challenge contemporary students like never before (Järvelä, Näykki, Laru, & Luokkanen, 2007). This change, however, requires student support and services to be reenvisioned to account for the increasingly online and hybridized nature of education (Dare, Zapata, & Thomas, 2005). Higher education leaders, specifically student affairs educators, are leading the exploration of more meaningful student technology applications and support services as these tools become increasingly pervasive (Cabellon, 2016; Ellison, Steinfield, & Lampe, 2011; Kuk, 2012). Being able to harness these technologies as they evolve becomes of critical importance to the forward-looking educator.

Recommendations for Effective Technology Use by Educators

Technology is in flux and evolving, requiring educators and students to continuously reexamine, remix, and adapt to change. Even as of the publication of this volume, technology and how educators use this technology may have shifted. The actual technological tools used, however, are less important than *how* they are used and what outcomes they attempt to achieve.

The preceding content provides a broad overview of the current state of technology and its impact on issues related to student leadership and leadership education. Concluding this chapter are recommendations for how to be an effective educator when incorporating and using digital tools in the educational environment. To that end, effective leadership educators:

1. *Engage in constant education and reeducation around the latest technologies, issues, and trends.* Students are looking to educators for help in understanding how to use new technologies to enhance their learning. One third of undergraduate students in the United States reported that they wished they were better prepared to use basic software applications prior to college, and nearly half reported that they wished they had better preparation to use learning management and related software (Dahlstrom et al., 2015). To best partner with students, educators themselves need to be fluent in new technologies and be able to teach students how to use these technologies.

2. *Develop infrastructures that support access to technology for all.* As technological competence increasingly becomes a requirement as opposed to an add-on for digital leaders, investments must be made in ensuring adequate infrastructures are in place to ensure access and encourage the use of technology. This includes basic Internet and technological device access as well as institutional operating policies that provide guidance and support for technology. This work of ensuring basic access should occur centrally and be assumed for an entire school or educational unit.

3. *Advocate for resources and deploy technologies that ensure students and fellow educators are able to access the latest tools and use them effectively.* In order to remain current with technological adoption and innovation in use, educators and administrators must dedicate the requisite human and financial resources to create the infrastructures needed to support technology within their programs. Furthermore, school and university leaders must build cultures that encourage active experimentation with technology and reward innovative practice (Kolomitz & Cabellon, 2016).

4. *Focus on evidence-based practice when deploying technology into learning environments while continuing to experiment with new technologies.* New technologies, applications, and tools are constantly being introduced. Effective digital leadership educators need to be wary of technologies that might be trendy or destined for the "junkyard of next big things" (Barr, McClennan, & Sandeen, 2014, p. 90) while continuing to experiment and innovate. Pilot programs and new technology deployments should be evaluated for impact and effectiveness through various empirical and assessment measures and may involve ongoing professional development and the creation of scholar-practitioner communities of practice (Blimling, 2001).

5. *Collaborate across traditional administrative silos and institutional boundaries.* Educators must build cross-divisional partnerships between staff members in information technology, marketing and communication, and in student and academic affairs units because technology is a shared responsibility (Bess & Dee, 2012). As Jones, Harper, and Schuh (2010) argued, "Now perhaps more than ever, our future depends on our ability to collaborate with multiple stakeholders and constituencies both public and private, and within and outside of our formalized educational environments" (p. 542).

6. *Aid students in navigating the new realities brought forward by digital and social media technologies—including issues of digital citizenship and leadership.* New digital and social technologies are not just tools; they also create environments and community spaces in which one can interact with others. Navigating the "new rules" of these environments requires individuals who understand how cultures develop online, how these online spaces and communities work, and how to act ethically and with purpose (Gismondi, 2015; Qualman, 2015). Leadership education that infuses digital technologies must account for these new realities as well as the developmental capacities student leaders need to navigate these spaces.

7. *Use (and teach others how to use) digital and social technologies for civic engagement and enacting social change.* New technologies, particularly social networking sites and social media, are changing the way people share information and organize themselves (Shirky, 2009). These changes have democratized the flow of information and changed the way traditional student leadership organizations function (Gismondi, 2015). Rather than be passive observers to this change, leadership educators can help student leaders use technological tools toward these ends more effectively.

8. *Model effective ways of integrating technology into one's life and leadership.* Although technology holds much promise for what it can help humans achieve, society must also make choices as to how and when technology should be used. Individuals must make choices as to how they want to integrate technology into their own lives, work, and leadership endeavors. Leadership educators can model the way by encouraging educators and students alike to think critically about how they communicate online and how it represents themselves, their peers, and the organizations of which they are a part. Finally, educators can encourage reflection and dialogue about the role technology can and should play in our lives.

Conclusion

Digital and social technologies are having a significant impact on the student experience and require educators to evolve and acquire new knowledge, skills, and competencies in order to remain relevant and effective. Digitally savvy students and educators have the power to reimagine traditional paradigms and develop new strategies for enacting social change, but only if they work together to understand the impact of these emerging technologies. To achieve this, an appreciation for technology's evolution and its individual and societal impact is required. Both educators and students must also continue to evolve alongside the technological tools they use to ensure these tools are used for purposeful productive ends. Remixing current student leadership programs to intentionally include digital technology can help ensure this (Ahlquist, 2015). Given the complexity of this task and the size and scope of leadership programs, the remainder of this volume specifically shares how leadership educators can achieve their goals.

References

ACPA: College Student Educators International, & NASPA: Student Affairs Administrators in Higher Education. (2015). *ACPA/ NASPA professional competency areas for student affairs practitioners* (2nd ed.). Washington, DC: Authors.

Ahlquist, J. (2015). *Developing digital student leaders: A mixed methods study of student leadership, identity, and decision making on social media* (Doctoral dissertation). Retrieved from ProQuest Dissertations and Theses. (Accession Order No. 3713711)

Barr, M. J., McClennan, G. S., & Sandeen, A. (2014). *Making change happen in student affairs.* New York, NY: Wiley.

Bess, J. L., & Dee, J. R. (2012). *Understanding college and university organizations: Theories for effective policy and practice, Vol. 2: Dynamics of the system.* Sterling, VA: Stylus.

Blimling, G. S. (2001). Uniting scholarship and communities of practice. *Journal of College Student Development, 42,* 381–396.

Bowen, W. G. (2013). *Higher education in the digital age.* Princeton, NJ: Princeton University Press.

boyd, d. m., & Ellison, N. B. (2007). Social networking sites: Definition, history, and scholarship. *Journal of Computer-Mediated Communication, 13,* 210–230.

Brown, M. G., Wohn, D. Y., & Ellison, N. (2016). Without a map: College access the online practice of youth from low-income communities. *Computers & Education, 92,* 104–116.

Brown, P. G. (2016). *College students, social media, digital identities, and the digitized self* (Doctoral dissertation). Retrieved from ProQuest Dissertations and Theses. (Accession Order No. 1776598125)

Cabellon, E. T. (2016). *Redefining student affairs through digital technology: A ten-year historiography of digital technology use by student affairs administrators* (Doctoral dissertation). Retrieved from ProQuest Dissertations and Theses. (Accession Order No. 10013238)

Cabellon, E. T., & Junco, R. (2015). The digital age of student affairs. In E. Whitt & J. Schuh (Eds.), *New Directions for Student Services: No. 15. New Directions for Student Services 1997–2014: Glancing back, looking forward* (pp. 49–61). San Francisco, CA: Jossey-Bass.

Chen, P. D., Lambert, A. D., & Guidry, K. R. (2010). Engaging online learners: The impact of Web-based learning technologies on college student engagement. *Computers & Education, 54,* 1222–1232.

Dahlstrom, E., Brooks, D. C., Grajek, S., & Reeves, J. (2015). *ECAR study of undergraduate students and information technology, 2015.* Louisville, CO: ECAR. Retrieved from http://net.educause.edu/ir/library/pdf/ss15/ers1510ss.pdf

Dalton, J. C. (2007). Concluding observations and implications of e-portfolios for student affairs leadership and programming. In J. Garis & J. Dalton (Eds.), *New Directions for Student Services: No. 119. e-Portfolios: Emerging opportunities for student affairs* (pp. 99–106). San Francisco, CA: Jossey-Bass.

Dare, L. A., Zapata, L. P., & Thomas, A. G. (2005). Assessing the needs of distance learners: A student affairs perspective. In K. Kruger (Ed.), *New Directions for Student Services: No. 112. Technology in student affairs: Supporting student learning and services* (pp. 39–54). San Francisco, CA: Jossey-Bass.

Ditzler, C., Hong, E., & Strudler, N. (2016). How tablets are utilized in the classroom. *Journal of Research on Technology in Education, 48,* 1–13.

Duggan, M. (2015, August 19). Mobile messaging and social media 2015. *Pew Research Center.* Retrieved from http://www.pewinternet.org/2015/08/19/mobile-messaging-and-social-media-2015/

Dunlap, J. C., & Lowenthal, P. R. (2009). Tweeting the night away: Using Twitter to enhance a social presence. *Journal of Information Systems Education, 20,* 129–136.

Eaton, P. (2015). *#Becoming: Emergent identity of college students in the digital age examined through complexivist epistemologies* (Doctoral dissertation). Baton Rouge, LA: Louisiana State University.

Ellison, N. B., Steinfield, C., & Lampe, C. (2011). Connection strategies: Social capital implications of Facebook-enabled communication practices. *New Media & Society, 13*(6), 873–892.

Gikas, J., & Grant, M. M. (2013). Mobile computing devices in higher education: Student perspectives on learning with cellphones, smartphones & social media. *The Internet and Higher Education, 19,* 18–26.

Gismondi, A. (2015). *#CivicEngagement: An exploratory study of social media use and civic engagement among undergraduates* (Doctoral dissertation). Chestnut Hill, MA: Boston College.

Grey, R., Vitak, J., Easton, E. W., & Ellison, N. B. (2013). Examining social adjustment to college in the age of social media: Factors influencing successful transitions and persistence. *Computers & Education, 67,* 193–207. doi:10.1016/j.compedu.2013.02.021

Harvard Business Review. (2010). *The new conversation: Taking social media from talk to action.* Boston, MA: Harvard Business School.

Hassan, M., & Geys, B. (2016). Who should pick up the bill? Distributing the financial burden of technological innovations in schools. *Computers & Education, 94,* 193–203.

Heiberger, G., & Harper, R. (2008). Have you Facebooked Astin lately? Using technology to increase student involvement. In R. Junco & D. M. Timm (Eds.), *New Directions for Student Services: No. 124. Using emerging technologies to enhance student engagement* (pp. 19–35). San Francisco, CA: Jossey-Bass.

International Society for Technology in Education. (2007). *ISTE standards for students.* Retrieved from http://www.iste.org/standards/iste-standards/standards-for-students

Järvelä, S., Näykki, P., Laru, J., & Luokkanen, T. (2007). Structuring and regulating collaborative learning in higher education with wireless networks and mobile tools. *Educational Technology & Society, 10*(4), 71–79.

Jones, S. R., Harper, S. R., & Schuh, J. H. (2010). Shaping the future. In J. Schuh, S. Jones, & S. Harper (Eds.), *Student services: A handbook for the profession* (pp. 535–547). San Francisco, CA: Jossey-Bass.

Joosten, T. (2012). *Social media for educators: Strategies and best practices.* New York, NY: Wiley.

Junco, R. (2014). *Engaging students through social media: Evidence based practices for use in student affairs.* San Francisco, CA: Jossey-Bass.

Kay, R. H., & Lauricella, S. (2011). Unstructured vs. structured use of laptops in higher education. *Journal of Information Technology Education: Innovations in Practice, 10*, 33–42.

Kim, M. K., Kim, S. M., Khera, O., & Getman, J. (2014). The experience of three flipped classrooms in an urban university: An exploration of design principles. *Internet and Higher Education, 22*, 37–50.

Kolomitz, K., & Cabellon, E. T. (2016). A strategic necessity: Building senior leadership's fluency in digital technology. In E. Cabellon & J. Ahlquist (Eds.), *New Directions for Student Services: No. 155. Engaging the digital generation* (pp. 47–57). San Francisco, CA: Jossey-Bass.

Kuk, L. (2012). The changing nature of student affairs. In A. Tull & L. Kuk (Eds.), *New realities in the management of student affairs* (pp. 3–12). Sterling, VA: Stylus.

Lederman, D., & Jaschik, S. (2013, August 27). Survey on faculty attitudes of technology. *Inside Higher Ed.* Retrieved from https://www.insidehighered.com/news/survey/survey-faculty-attitudes-technology

Logan, T. J. (2015). *An investigation of twitter interactions amongst newly admitted college students at a large public institution* (Doctoral dissertation). Retrieved from ProQuest Dissertations and Theses. (Accession Order No 10102503)

Matias, A., & Wolf, D. F. (2013). Engaging students in online courses through the use of mobile technology. *Cutting-edge Technologies in Higher Education, 6*, 115–142.

McWilliams, J., Hickey, D. T., Hines, M. B., Conner, J. M., & Bishop, S. C. (2011). Using collaborative writing tools for literary analysis: Twitter, fan fiction and the crucible in the secondary English classroom. *Journal of Media Literacy Education, 2*(3), 238–245.

Perrin, A., & Duggan, M. (2015, June 26). Americans' internet access: 2000–2015. *Pew Research Center.* Retrieved from http://www.pewinternet.org/2015/06/26/americans-internet-access-2000-2015/

Qualman, E. (2015). *What happens on campus stays on YouTube.* Cambridge, MA: Equalman Studios.

Roberts-Mahoney, H., Means, A. J., & Garrison, M. J. (2016). Netflixing human capital development: Personalized learning technology and the corporatization of K–12 education. *Journal of Education Policy, 31*(4), 405–420.

Shirky, C. (2009). *Here comes everybody: The power of organizing without organizations.* New York, NY: Penguin.

Spitzer, B., Morel, V., Buvat, J., & Subrahmanyam, K. V. J. (2013). *The digital talent gap: Developing skills for today's digital organizations.* Capgemini Consulting. Retrieved from https://www.capgemini.com/resource-file-access/resource/pdf/the_digital_talent_gap27-09_0.pdf

Wankel, C., & Blessinger, P. (2013). *Increasing student engagement and retention in e-learning environments: Web 2.0 and blended learning technologies* (Vol. 6). Somerville, MA: Emerald Group Publishing.

EDMUND T. CABELLON *is the assistant to the vice president of student affairs and enrollment management at Bridgewater State University and the former cochair of ACPA's presidential task force on digital technology. He is a senior student affairs administrator, speaker, and writer leading higher education through strategic application of digital technology and communication tools.*

PAUL GORDON BROWN *is the director of curriculum, training, and research for the higher educational software company, Roompact. He is also an independent speaker and consultant on social and digital technology's impact on contemporary college student learning and development.*

2

Technological innovation has become a driver of educational and leadership development practices that place students at the center of learning and leadership development experiences.

Leadership 2.0: The Impact of Technology on Leadership Development

John L. Hoffman, Cara Vorhies

Students live, learn, and develop in virtual as well as physical contexts. When working with a generation that is more—although not fully— digitally astute, efforts to separate the two are typically counterproductive. In spite of this, educators in and out of the classroom too often draw hard distinctions between face-to-face and online learning contexts. Even writers who espouse greater digital integration with language such as "technology-enhanced education" (e.g., Khatib, 2014; Shand, Winstead, & Kottler, 2012) implicitly norm face-to-face instruction and imply that technology is an add-on or enhancement. To this point, Laurillard (2013) noted,

> We tend to use technology to support traditional modes of teaching— improving the quality of lecture presentations using interactive whiteboards, making lecture notes readable in PowerPoint and available online, extending the library by providing access to digital resources and libraries, recreating face-to-face tutorial discussions asynchronously online–all of them good, incremental improvements in quality and flexibility, but nowhere near being transformational. (pp. xix–xx)

Laurillard later argued that to become transformational, educators must reexamine their work through the lens of the learner, including the learner's orientation toward technology.

The paradigm shift placing the learner at the center of educational practice has implications for the field of leadership development as well as for educational practice; thus, our title "Leadership 2.0." Rosen (2008) noted the shift from Web 1.0 to 2.0 was from a read-only environment to a read-write ecology in which learners publish content, engage in social

NEW DIRECTIONS FOR STUDENT LEADERSHIP, no. 153, Spring 2017 © 2017 Wiley Periodicals, Inc., A Wiley Company
Published online in Wiley Online Library (wileyonlinelibrary.com) • DOI: 10.1002/yd.20227

networking, and develop community. In a Web 1.0 context, educators used the Internet to access information or to augment traditional instruction. With the emergence of Web 2.0, the Internet has become an environmental context or ecosystem in which humans interact with one another (Luckin, 2008; Rosen, 2008). This ecology implies the potential for development (Bronfenbrenner, 1989), and we argue this includes the development of leadership knowledge, skills, and dispositions. More specifically, we propose new 2.0 conceptions of education and leadership in which educators and students, as well as leaders and followers, must engage in read-write efforts to create organizations and communities of action that are inclusive and integrative of physical and virtual contexts.

Central to this work are implications for equitable and inclusive educational practice. Although emergent technologies have improved the quality of education for many students, not all students have equitable access to these technologies. Though these technologies have potential to narrow disparities in achievement (Vigdor, Ladd, & Martinez, 2014; Walton, Kop, Spriggs, & Fitzgerald, 2013), they have more often contributed to growing opportunity gaps along lines of race, gender, and socioeconomic status (Goode, 2010). Although a full discussion of the connections between digital divides, opportunity gaps, and achievement extends beyond the scope and purpose of this chapter, we attend to means by which emergent instructional and educational practices can be just and inclusive in terms of process as well as outcomes in the training and development of leaders.

In this chapter, our aim is to explore the efficacy of leadership development theory and practices that integrate physical and virtual spaces. We begin with a discussion of shifts in emergent instructional approaches that have been influenced by technological advancements in education—approaches that are integrative of physical and virtual spaces. This discussion includes specific attention to educational practices that extend beyond the classroom and that are equitable and socially just. We intentionally use the term "educator" as inclusive of both classroom instructors and professionals such as student affairs educators who work outside the classroom, but with a central focus on learning (ACPA: College Student Educators International & NASPA: Student Affairs Administrators in Higher Education, 2015). Next, we connect this approach to recent work that has addressed leadership development theory and applications to practice. This leads to our final section in which we present implications for theory-informed leadership development practices that use technology and span physical and virtual spaces.

Education in Virtual and Physical Contexts

We begin by reviewing changes in instructional theory that have accompanied technological shifts from Web 1.0 to Web 2.0. This serves as a basis

NEW DIRECTIONS FOR STUDENT LEADERSHIP • DOI: 10.1002/yd

for later content addressing similar shifts in leadership development theory and practice.

Background: Andragogy and Self-Directed Learning.   Early applications of online education were set in a Web 1.0 context and were viewed by many as an extension of distance education by correspondence or television, largely with adult learners. Perhaps for this reason, early theoretical foundations for computer-based education were grounded in methods of teaching adults or andragogy (Lauzon, 1992; Rossman, 2000) and self-directed learning (Lieberman, 1991; Seaton, 1993). Merriam, Caffarella, and Baumgartner (2007) reviewed the self-directed learning literature and noted that a central goal for many authors was "to promote emancipatory learning and social action as an integral part of self-directed learning" (p. 107). However, there is little evidence that computer-based self-directed learning efforts achieved this goal. Merriam et al. (2007) noted that self-directed learning applications may have placed an over-reliance on the mastery of content and skills for specific, self-directed purposes rather than extending to an "examination by learners of the sociopolitical assumptions under which they learn and function, [and] also the incorporation of collective action as an outcome" (p. 108). Similarly, Collins (1996) remarked that self-directed learning could "condition the individual into taken-for-granted acceptance of what is offered" (p. 115).

Self-Determined Learning.   More recent writings that are inclusive of contemporary technologies such as Web 2.0 and social media have moved learners of all ages further to the center of the educational experience. Hase and Kenyon (2000, 2007) described this approach as self-*determined* learning or, more formally, as heutagogy. More so than with the case of self-*directed* learning and andragogy, self-determined learning and heutagogy have been used interchangeably in the literature. Hase and Kenyon (2007) stated that in heutagogy, learners are "the major agent in their own learning, which occurs as a result of personal experiences" (p. 112). Blaschke (2012) noted, "Heutagogy applies to a holistic approach to developing learner capabilities" (p. 58) in which "the instructor … facilitates the learning process by providing guidance and resources, but fully relinquishes ownership of the learning path and process to the learner" (p. 59). Thus, the educator serves as a guide to learners who establish their own learning outcomes, design learning experiences, assume responsibility for implementation, and both craft assessment strategies and interpret the results. The impact of this shift has been evident even with young learners as pedagogical practices influenced by Common Core State Standards (CCSS) challenge educators to encourage students to choose problems of interest and find multiple ways of solving those problems and then ask learners which approaches worked best for them. Notably, the International Society for Technology in Education (ISTE) stated the following regarding the ISTE standards and the CCSS:

When we all have anytime, anywhere access to a universe of facts, an emphasis on top-down knowledge delivery and rote memorization no longer makes sense. Instead, we must embrace new pedagogies that make the most of our students' innate drive to learn, create, and collaborate. The ISTE Standards share with the Common Core an emphasis on using technology—not for technology's sake, but as a tool for leap-frogging over lower-order thinking skills, such as rote memorization, to focus our energies on research and media literacy, creativity, collaboration, problem solving, and critical thinking. (ISTE, n.d., para. 2–3)

This should be empowering to educators because it eases the burden of mastering lower order "how to" skills associated with new and changing technologies. Instead, educators attend to higher order aspects of the learning process and ensure that learning spans both physical and virtual contexts. Imagine, for example, an educator facilitating the development of basic leadership skills by asking students to promote an event using both physical and virtual technologies. Just as the learners may have a better sense of where to place posters within their home community in order to draw the most attention, they may have a better understanding of which forms of social media best fit with the event and its target audiences. Though educators would benefit from a foundational understanding of the technologies used, their primary responsibility is guiding the learning process—outcomes, design, implementation, and assessment. Similarly, leaders of large organizations may benefit from a basic understanding of the various technical aspects of the organization's work, but they delegate primary responsibility for those aspects to managers while they focus on higher order questions of mission, strategic planning and implementation, and ongoing evaluation and improvement.

To fully appreciate the potential of self-determined learning for using technology in leadership development, two additional concepts from the heutagogy literature require attention. The first is "double-loop learning", which was originally introduced by Argyris and Schön (1974) in their writings addressing organizational learning. In single-loop learning, managers (i.e., leaders) define the problem, take action, consider the outcomes, and then return to their understanding of the problem, which leads to new action and so forth. Double-loop learning retains the single-loop process but adds a second loop in which leaders (or educators) examine their beliefs and actions between the considering outcomes and revisiting the problem. Senge (1990) referred to this process as "surfacing mental models" (p. 14), meaning that leaders must actively and systematically explore values, biases, and habits of the mind embedded within the subconscious by bringing them to consciousness where individuals can act upon them. In our previous example, students might do a great job promoting the event via social media in terms of the problem and action but fail to examine deeper assumptions. For instance, students might believe their target audience uses the same social media they do or that the role of social media is solely for publicity rather than also for contributing to design, delivery, and evaluation of the event. In a self-determined learning paradigm, educators focus greater attention on helping learners surface their mental models rather than for any technical aspect of the learning experience.

Another concept addressed within the heutagogy literature is the distinction between competency and capability. Blaschke (2012) summarized these two concepts as follows:

> When learners are competent, they demonstrate the acquisition of knowledge and skills; skills can be repeated and knowledge retrieved. When learners are capable, skills and knowledge can be reproduced in unfamiliar situations. Capability is then the extension of one's own competence, and without competency there cannot be capability. Through the double-looping, learners become more aware of their preferred learning style and can easily adapt new learning situations to learning styles, thus making them more capable learners. (p. 60)

Once again, we return to our prior example. High school or college-age students might develop high-level competency in designing, promoting, implementing, and evaluating events for ethnically diverse peers. The work of leadership educators must go a step further to ensure that those competencies develop into broader capabilities so that, upon graduation, students are able to scale up transferable skills in order to work with audiences that are diverse in terms of age as well as ethnicity or other dimensions of diversity.

Moving beyond leadership competency to leadership capability is critical in technologically rich contexts that evolve quickly. Consider an example from social media. With horizontal shifts over time from AOL Instant Messenger to texting and other applications, or from Myspace to Facebook, technological *competencies* were sufficient as the platform differences largely had to do with format and user preferences. However, vertical shifts from messaging tools to Facebook, and later from Facebook to Twitter, Snapchat, or Yik Yak, each required deeper *capabilities* as users had to apply and expand knowledge, skills, and dispositions in unfamiliar virtual environments that made new assumptions about users, identities, and privacy. From the perspective of an educator, once a student demonstrates capability to move vertically, say from WeChat to Instagram to Snapchat, the educator should have increased confidence that this same student will have the capability needed to move to the next generations of social media applications that emerge.

Implications for Practices That Are Inclusive and Socially Just.   Attention to practices that are inclusive and socially just have received minimal attention in the leadership development literature (Kodama & Dugan, 2013; Ospina & Foldy, 2009) as well as in literature addressing the use of technology in education (Merriam et al., 2007; Selwyn, 2010). Within a self-determined learning framework, there is certainly potential for students in poorly implemented learning experiences to fail to consider deeper, social justice outcomes. That being said, we suggest that strong self-determined learning experiences are particularly well suited for achieving social justice outcomes as well as leadership development outcomes because of the central role afforded to students.

We suggested previously that educators should relinquish their responsibility for enhancing education with technology and instead learn from students how they intuitively and instinctively navigate virtual and physical spaces. Most—though not all—millennial generation students in the United States have grown up with virtual spaces as a natural component of their broader ecology. One might also say that virtual realities are a part of their shared culture. When educators teach lessons or facilitate learning experiences related to the content of cultures other than their own, they must do so with significant care and humility. Self-determined learning approaches open greater space for students to assume responsibility for bringing the content from their multiple, intersecting identities and cultures to the learning experience. The educator maintains responsibility for ensuring that diverse members within a learning community be allowed to define and solve the same problem in different ways, to different ends, and in a manner that honors their intersecting cultures and identities. Content-related questions of accuracy and precision (questions that often carry greater weight within the dominant culture) are not surrendered but evaluated by diverse students drawing upon their own cultures. In relation to both the intersection of physical and virtual spaces and the interaction of students from diverse cultures, the educator's focus is on the second loop of the learning process—ensuring that deeper assumptions and values about space, culture, and community are surfaced, considered, and acted upon. Further, a central duty of the educator is to ensure that learning experiences are inclusive of students outside the dominant culture—including those millennial generation students who grew up with limited access to technology.

To summarize, the shift of Web 1.0 to Web 2.0 has been marked by movement toward a read-write ecology. This shift is evident in self-determined learning approaches as educators do more than write and learners do more than read. Instead, educators and learners collaborate in learning experiences, each engaging in read-write aspects of the process. Further, educators focus on higher order questions of (a) process (outcome, design, implementation, and evaluation); (b) double-loop learning and surfacing mental models including models that are informed by culture and multiple, intersecting identities; and (c) movement from competency development to capability development among learners. A similar shift is evident in the move to Leadership 2.0 as leaders must engage in read-write interactions with followers while focusing on higher order questions of process, surfacing underlying individually held and organizational assumptions, and movement from organizational competency to organizational capability. In the next section, we present a model of leadership development that we believe is particularly useful for educators working with school- and college-age youth. We then propose adaptations and extensions of this model that reflect a Leadership 2.0 orientation that spans virtual and physical spaces. Finally, we use this as the basis for discussing technologically rich and integrative educational practices that facilitate leadership development within a Leadership 2.0 context.

Leadership Development Theory in the Digital Age: A Selected Model

Komives, Longerbeam, Owen, Mainella, and Osteen (2006) conducted a grounded theory investigation of the developmental progression of college students' leadership identity development (LID) with the express purpose of informing educational practices that can facilitate such development. The resulting multifaceted model that emerged included a six-stage progression of students' views of leadership. The first two stages reflect largely dualistic, dependent orientations toward leadership, and the third begins to mark a shift toward a subjective stance, though still with an outward focus. In the first stage, *awareness*, students view others rather than themselves as leaders, particularly authority figures in formally defined positions. In the second stage of the model, *exploration and engagement*, the view of leadership does not shift much, but students demonstrate an interest in becoming involved and wanting to do more. It is worthwhile to note here that involvement in physical spaces is typically biased toward extroverted individuals. As Amichai-Hamburger, Wainapel, and Fox (2004) noted in the title of their study of personality type and engagement, "On the Internet, no one knows I'm an introvert" (p. 125). Virtual spaces have the capacity to expand involvement opportunities and for educators to identify potential leaders who likely would have been missed in physical spaces. This more inclusive approach to who becomes involved may then influence the third stage, *leader identified*, in which students begin to view leaders as the people who get things done rather than those who hold titles.

The fourth stage of the model, *leadership differentiated*, marks an important shift toward agency on the part of students. Holding on to the belief that leadership is about getting things done, students begin to explore their own role in how groups work together to accomplish change. In light of our discussion thus far, this is where a read-write orientation emerges. It also contrasts 2.0 approaches to leadership from 1.0 theory that often focused on the work of a singular leader. It is no coincidence that much of the formal leadership theory that has emerged in the 2.0 era is more participatory in its orientation (e.g., Hoch & Kozlowski, 2014; Thomas, Martin, & Riggio, 2013). In the fifth stage of *generativity*, student leaders build on their participatory orientation from the fourth stage with greater commitment and effort to develop the leadership potential of other students within their groups. This is consistent not only with a 2.0 orientation but also with the tenets of self-determined learning theory as the process of facilitating leadership development in others is a practice that should help leaders to move beyond leadership competence to leadership capability. Finally, in the sixth stage of *integration and synthesis*, students demonstrate and integrate a leadership identity.

Applications of Technology to Leadership Development Practice

Whereas Komives et al. (2006) presented preliminary applications to practice for their LID model, Komives, Longerbeam, Mainella, Osteen, and Owen (2009) extended this work with a more in-depth discussion of the opportunities and challenges in applying the model. Komives et al. (2009) applied Bandura's (1997) four sources or antecedents for the development of efficacy as a framework for their applications of LID: (a) mastery experiences, (b) vicarious experiences, (c) verbal persuasion, and (d) physiological and affective states. We focus on the first two of these four. Their application is especially relevant as Blaschke (2012) identified their connection to the development of efficacy as a central to helping individuals extend *competencies* (including leadership competencies) from one context to another as *capabilities*. For our purposes, we are primarily concerned with physical and virtual contexts, which, as noted from the onset of this chapter, many students experience in a highly integrated manner.

The range of mastery experiences in leadership development is quite broad. We focus on three: (a) experiential team-building exercises, (b) student government and leadership roles, and (c) vicarious learning experiences. On the surface, these types of programs may imply physical contexts. By moving students to the center of self-determined learning experiences, there is significant potential to reimagine and redesign these types of experiences. Consider the following experiential team-building possibilities:

- Scavenger hunts can be spread across virtual spaces (such as websites or blogs) as well as physical spaces. Evidence of scavenged items can be collected with digital cameras and reported using various social media platforms.
- "Amazing race" exercises can be enlarged to span virtual and physical spaces. Clues can be posted to hidden hashtags on Twitter that are discovered once various "destinations" are reached by team members, potentially communicated to other members through different platforms such as Snapchat or Instagram.
- Physically based "ropes course" activities can be augmented with communications shared via electronic text or images rather than orally.

NEW DIRECTIONS FOR STUDENT LEADERSHIP • DOI: 10.1002/yd

As suggested previously, the primary role of the educator is to attend to process, especially to double-loop learning involving the surfacing of mental and cultural ways of knowing and to extend increases in competency into capability development that spans multiple contexts and situations. Students bring their cultural knowledge—including working knowledge of various technologies—to the learning experiences.

Student government and student leadership roles with clubs and organizations are also strong leadership development experiences that can be reimagined in ways that are more inclusive of virtual spaces. Beginning with its 10th edition published in 2000, *Robert's Rules of Order* began to include footnotes acknowledging synchronistic and nonsynchronistic meetings (Robert, Honemann, Balch, Evans, & Robert, 2000). Shortly thereafter, members of the American Institute of Parliamentarians and the National Association of Parliamentarians began issuing guidelines for e-meetings and e-voting (Stackpole, 2001; Sylvester, 2000, 2001). The guidelines address a variety of meeting types (such as email, chat rooms, and video conferencing) as well as a range of issues including establishing a quorum, motions and discussion, and voting. These are relevant not only because virtual meetings are sure to increase in frequency in the future but also because of their implications for participatory governance. Student governments, organizations, and clubs have long bemoaned difficulties in securing participation from their constituents. This is especially true for students who commute to schools or colleges and for those from low-income families with high work demands for the students or their parents. On their own, e-meetings will not remedy these concerns, but they present an opportunity for a critical discussion regarding how to lead in ways that are inclusive and equitable. Further, expanding opportunities for involvement broadens the base for later leadership development in the LID model.

Vicarious experiences are those through which students develop a sense of engagement by observing the activities of others with whom they identify. At their most basic level, vicarious experiences can consist of personal stories shared by educators or mentors. Movies, videos, and YouTube clips are commonly used media tools through which students engage in a learning experience vicariously through their observations of others. The applications to self-determined learning approaches to leadership development are rather straightforward. Leadership receives ample coverage by all forms of media, and the volume of vicarious experiences for students to choose from is near limitless. In terms of double-loop learning, educators should focus on media literacy by surfacing questions about accuracy as well as the motives and values of those who created the media. Furthermore, whereas certain views of leadership are privileged within media as within the broader culture, progressive educators can infuse examples of leadership enacted by women; people of color; and the lesbian, gay, bisexual, and trans* community. With thoughtful coaching on the part of educators, students can design learning experiences that surface the underlying mental models and cultural values of various leaders, thus preparing them to better consider the influence of their own intersecting identities on their approach to leadership.

For these three sets of activities, the LID model provides tangible direction to educators regarding their work with self-determined, leadership-focused mastery experiences. Within the first three stages of the LID, the developmental steps consist of first getting students involved and then identifying who assumes responsibility for getting things done. In addition to creating spaces that stimulate greater involvement by both introverted and extroverted students (Amichai-Hamburger et al., 2004), the technologies and virtual contexts often provide a record of the activity. During the reflection components of experiential learning, students can review activity records to see who was involved and how (e.g., virtual meeting transcripts and minutes, social media feeds). In physical contexts, group memory often privileges extroverted individuals who are articulate in the moment, but technology may help to identify other students who played a significant role in getting things done, albeit in a less outgoing or charismatic manner. This can serve to broaden the base of those perceived as potential leaders and behaviors that promote leadership among group members regardless of positional role.

In the later LID stages, developmental shifts involve individuals who identified as leaders getting others involved, building their capacity for leadership, and ultimately individuals identifying leadership as an integral part of their identity. Again, technological records of activities could prove valuable to reflective learning but with greater attention to deeper learning processes. As educators focus on double-loop learning and surfacing mental models, deeper questions emerge that go beyond who was involved and how. At this level, one can consider why various individuals or groups were more or less involved or why they engaged in the process in different ways. For example, educators may ask students to review online activity records with the goal of identifying the values and norms of the group's interactions. Debriefing questions might include the following:

- Are the values and norms consistent across physical and virtual contexts?
- How did group interactions welcome or privilege some individuals while leaving others out or minimizing and marginalizing their perspectives?
- Once individuals become involved, are they afforded space to act as leaders and influence larger group work?

These types of questions can involve greater risk to participants, especially if technological records include examples of participant behavior that go against the desired group norms for physical and virtual spaces. Thus, educators may wish to begin with safer vicarious experiences in which students identify examples of leadership and group interactions from various media sources, and then identify norms, values, and privileging behaviors in those media examples. Once students have engaged in the practice of uncovering and examining underlying values of others through vicarious experiences, educators may invite them to engage in similar practices considering records of their own activities online.

Conclusion

We began this chapter with the assertion that students live, learn, and develop in virtual as well as physical contexts. Given 1.0 to 2.0 shifts, students now expect read-write ecologies. We see this as an opportunity for enhancing leadership development efforts as student leaders assume greater responsibility for the design, implementation, and evaluation of their learning experiences whereas leadership educators focus on surfacing mental models and moving from competency to capability. Further, leadership educators can afford greater attention to ensuring the leadership development experiences are inclusive, equitable, and socially just.

References

ACPA: College Student Educators International, & NASPA: Student Affairs Administrators in Higher Education. (2015). *Professional competency areas for student affairs educators*. Washington, DC: Authors.

Amichai-Hamburger, Y., Wainapel, G., & Fox, S. (2004). On the Internet no one knows I'm an introvert: Extroversion, neuroticism, and Internet interaction. *CyberPsychology & Behavior, 5*, 125–128.

Argyris, C., & Schön, D. (1974). *Theory in practice: Increasing professional effectiveness*. San Francisco, CA: Jossey-Bass.

Bandura, A. (1997). *Self-efficacy: The exercise of control*. New York, NY: Worth Publishers.

Blaschke, L. M. (2012). Heutagogy and lifelong learning: A review of heutagogical practice and self-determined learning. *International Review of Research in Open and Distance Learning, 13*(1), 56–71.

Bronfenbrenner, U. (1989). Ecological systems theory. In R. Vasta (Ed.), *Six theories of development* (pp. 187–249). Greenwich, CT: JAI Press.

Collins, M. (1996). On contemporary practice and research: Self-directed learning to critical theory. In R. Edwards, A. Hanson, & P. Raggatt (Eds.), *Boundaries of adult learning: Adult learners, education, and training* (pp. 109–127). New York, NY: Routledge.

Goode, J. (2010). Mind the gap: The digital dimension of college access. *Journal of Higher Education, 81*, 583–618.

Hase, S., & Kenyon, C. (2000). From andragogy to heutagogy. In *UltiBase Articles*. Retrieved from http://www.psy.gla.ac.uk/~steve/pr/Heutagogy.html

Hase, S., & Kenyon, C. (2007). Heutagogy: A child of complexity theory. *Complicity: An International Journal of Complexity and Education, 4*(1), 111–119.

Hoch, J. E., & Kozlowski, S. W. (2014). Leading virtual teams: Hierarchical leadership, structural supports, and shared team leadership. *Journal of Applied Psychology, 99*, 390–403.

International Society for Technology in Education. (n.d.). *ISTE standards and the common core*. Retrieved from http://www.iste.org/standards/standards-in-action/common-core

Khatib, N. M. (2014). The adoption of technology-enhanced instruction to support education for all. *Gifted and Talented International, 29*(1–2), 93–98.

Kodama, C. M., & Dugan, J. P. (2013). Leveraging leadership efficacy for college students: Disaggregating data to examine unique predictors by race. *Equity and Excellence in Education, 46*, 184–201. doi:10.1080/10665684.2013.780646

Komives, S. R., Longerbeam, S. D., Mainella, F., Osteen, L., & Owen, J. E. (2009). Leadership identity development: Challenges in applying a developmental model. *Journal of Leadership Education, 8*(1), 11–30.

Komives, S. R., Longerbeam, S. D., Owen, J. E., Mainella, F. C., & Osteen, L. (2006). A leadership identity development model: Applications from a grounded theory. *Journal of College Student Development, 47*, 401–442.

Laurillard, D. (2013). Foreword to the first edition. In H. Beetham, & R. Sharpe (Eds.), *Rethinking pedagogy for a digital age: Designing and delivering e-learning* (2nd ed., pp. xix–xxi). London, England: Routledge.

Lauzon, A. C. (1992). Integrating computer-based instruction with computer conferencing: An evaluation of a model for designing online education. *American Journal of Distance Education, 6*, 32–46.

Lieberman, D. A. (1991). Learning to learn revisited: Computers and the development of self-directed learning skills. *Journal of Research on Computing in Education, 23*, 373–395.

Luckin, R. (2008). The learner centric ecology of resources: A framework for using technology to scaffold learning. *Computers and Education, 50*, 449–462.

Merriam, S. B., Caffarella, R. S., & Baumgartner, L. M. (2007). *Learning in adulthood: A comprehensive guide* (3rd ed.). San Francisco, CA: Jossey-Bass.

Ospina, S., & Foldy, E. (2009). A critical review of race and ethnicity in the leadership literature: Surfacing context, power and the collective dimensions of leadership. *Leadership Quarterly, 20*, 876–896.

Robert, H. M., Honemann, D. H., Balch, T. J., Evans, W. J., & Robert, S. C. (2000). *Robert's rules of order: Newly revised* (10th ed.). Cambridge, MA: Perseus Publishing.

Rosen, S. (2008). Web 2.0.: A new generation of learners and education. *Computers in the Schools, 25*, 211–215.

Rossman, M. H. (2000). Andragogy and distance education: Together in the new millennium. *New Horizons in Adult Education and Human Resource Development, 14*(1), 4–11.

Seaton, W. J. (1993). Commuter-mediated communication and student self-directed learning. *Open Learning: The Journal of Open, Distance, and e-Learning, 8*, 49–54.

Selwyn, N. (2010). Looking beyond learning: Notes towards the critical study of educational technology. *Journal of Computer Assisted Learning, 26*, 65–73. doi: 10.1111/j.1365-2729.2009.00338.x

Senge, P. M. (1990). *The fifth discipline: The art and practice of the learning organization.* New York, NY: Doubleday.

Shand, K., Winstead, L., & Kottler, E. (2012). Journey to medieval China: Using technology-enhanced instruction to develop content knowledge and digital literacy skills. *Social Studies, 103*, 20–30.

Stackpole, J. D. (2001). The e-liberative assembly. *Parliamentary Journal, 42*(3), 81–95.

Sylvester, N. (2000). E-meetings: The future is now! *National Parliamentarian, 61*(2), 26–29.

Sylvester, N. (2001). E-meetings: The future is now! Part II. *National Parliamentarian, 62*(1), 30–31.

Thomas, G., Martin, R., & Riggio, R. E. (2013). Leading groups: Leadership as a group process. *Group Processes and Intergroup Relations, 16*, 3–16.

Vigdor, J. L., Ladd, H. F., & Martinez, E. (2014). Scaling the digital divide: Home computer technology and student achievement. *Economic Inquiry, 52*, 1103–1119.

Walton, P., Kop, T., Spriggs, D., & Fitzgerald, B. (2013). A digital inclusion: Empowering all Australians. *Australian Journal of Telecommunications and the Digital Economy, 1*(1), 9.1–9.17.

JOHN L. HOFFMAN *is the chair of the Department of Educational Leadership and the director of the Doctor of Educational Leadership Program at California State University, Fullerton. He chaired the subcommittee of the 2015 ACPA and NASPA Student Affairs Competencies Task Force that introduced "technology" as a competency area for student affairs educators.*

CARA VORHIES *is an English and Language Arts teacher at Norwalk High School in Norwalk, California. She also teaches as an adjunct instructor at Long Beach City College. Cara's dissertation research examined applications of self-determined learning to the Common Core State Standards and provided the theoretical foundation of this chapter.*

3

This chapter explores a P–20 digital citizenship model that builds upon the respect, educate, and protect REP model beginning with our earliest learners through elementary, middle, high school, and college.

P–20 Model of Digital Citizenship

Marialice B. F. X. Curran, Mike Ribble

With the onset of social media, multiple platforms, and apps, we are living in a networked environment that demands more focus on modeling and teaching a new way of connecting, communicating, collaborating, and learning than ever before. Common Sense Media recently published a report, *Technology Addiction: Concern, Controversy and Finding Balance* (2016), that stated:

> Over the past decade, society has witnessed changes in the way media and technology intersect with the ways we work and love. Devices are more mobile, functional, and seemingly indispensable. Accordingly, we've integrated media and technology into more and more of our lives, bringing devices with us everywhere and depending on them for a range of work, school, play, and social functions. (p. 5)

Learning in a connected society is mobile, immediate, social, and collaborative in nature; therefore, educating students, teachers, administrators, and even parents on the use of digital technologies is an opportunity for an entire community to participate in civil discourse. According to Ohler (2016), "Digital citizenship provides a real opportunity to rebuild our educational systems" (p. 53).

Because our lives are constantly evolving with upgrades and new ways to consume and produce electronic media, it should be no surprise that digital citizenship is a complicated term to define. Both the terms "digital" and "citizenship" are so broad (Ahlquist, 2016; Bearden, 2016; Ribble, 2011, 2015), complicating definitions even more. According to Douglas (2014), citizenship is defined as "personal, not legal. It is belonging to a nation or a community and contributing to that society's well-being" (p. 29). Now add digital to citizenship and the definition becomes even

NEW DIRECTIONS FOR STUDENT LEADERSHIP, no. 153, Spring 2017 © 2017 Wiley Periodicals, Inc., A Wiley Company
Published online in Wiley Online Library (wileyonlinelibrary.com) • DOI: 10.1002/yd.20228

harder to define. What is digital citizenship? Put simply it is the norms of appropriate, responsible behavior with regard to technology use (Douglas, 2014; Ribble, 2015). Digital citizenship is not just a set of rules of what can and cannot be done online. Instead, digital citizenship is a comprehensive look at how individuals actively solve problems and participate in online platforms, communities, and networks.

Understanding the significance and permanency of online choices affects how these choices intersect with our personal and professional lives at home, at school, and in our communities. Therefore, the ultimate goal is to help students of all ages to understand how to be personally responsible, participatory, and justice-oriented citizens both on and offline (Kahne, Chi, & Middaugh, 2006).

This chapter explores ways that elementary, middle, high schools, as well as colleges can embed digital citizenship into curriculum and instruction in order to prepare students at all levels to lead with empathy and respect, to create solutions and be problem solvers, and value the participatory nature of digital citizenship.

The Historical Context: Introducing Digital Citizenship

This chapter references nine elements of digital citizenship: digital access, digital commerce, digital communication, digital literacy, digital etiquette, digital law, digital rights and responsibilities, digital health and wellness, and digital security to describe the norms of appropriate, responsible behavior with regard to technology use (Ribble, 2015). As the options of how people communicate continue to change at such a rapid pace, these nine elements have been organized into three categories: respect, educate, and protect (REP; Ribble, 2015). Using the REP model can help schools develop and implement a P–20 digital citizenship curriculum. The principles of respect, educate, and protect include the nine digital citizenship elements to help educators, parents, and students discuss the issues that can be interwoven, built upon, and added to curriculum beginning with our youngest learners and continuing through college and beyond.

A P–20 Digital Citizenship Curriculum

What does digital citizenship look like and what does it mean to be a digital citizen? Just like being a citizen, a digital citizen is an active participant in an online community with a particular focus on creating solutions at a local, global, and digital level simultaneously (Curran, 2012). The ideal digital citizen is an active citizen; not just a resident, but an enabler of change (Curran, 2012). The REP model focuses on repeating the themes of respect, educate, and protect throughout the educational career of a student, in order to address the needs of being a digital citizen who is socially responsible, participatory in nature, and justice oriented (see Table 3.1).

NEW DIRECTIONS FOR STUDENT LEADERSHIP • DOI: 10.1002/yd

Table 3.1   Digital Citizenship Elements

Elements	REP Area	Cycle
Digital Etiquette	Respect	One—K–2
Digital Literacy	Educate	One—K–2
Digital Rights & Responsibilities	Protect	One—K–2
Digital Access	Respect	Two—3–5
Digital Communication	Educate	Two—3–5
Digital Safety	Protect	Two—3–5
Digital Law	Respect	Three—6–8
Digital Commerce	Educate	Three—6–8
Digital Health & Welfare	Protect	Three—6–8

Respect Yourself and Others.   The three digital citizenship elements that fit within the theme of respect are etiquette, access, and law. When addressing the element of *etiquette,* it is important to remember the "Golden Rule," especially with the anonymous nature of being online, which can often result in students forgetting the fact that a human being is behind that text, tweet, or post. Digital etiquette is a reminder to humanize the person next to us, as well as across the screen (Ribble, 2015). Etiquette for our youngest learners needs a focus on empathy, kindness, and how to be a friend both on and offline. As the theme of respect is repeated, etiquette will involve the online skills necessary to compose an email, write online comments on blog posts or social networking platforms, and use video platforms like Skype, Google Hangout, Periscope, and Blab in socially responsible and professional ways.

The second digital citizenship element in the respect category is *access.* The digital divide, a term that addresses a stark disparity between students who have access to technology and high-speed Internet and students who do not have access, looms heavy over educators, parents, and the federal government (Kang, 2016). Digital access does not just mean access to technology itself, but rather access to resources. In particular, digital access is the ability to interact with others in a users' world through a variety of digital and networking tools.

Issues surrounding access have been most commonly associated with physical, socioeconomic, and location dimensions (Ribble, 2015). Education institutions are faced with decisions to address this problem and provide equalization of technology and other access. For example, according to Coachella Valley Unified School District in California, 40% of their students do not have Internet access at home. To solve this problem, Superintendent Darryl Adams decided to park school buses with WiFi routers in neighborhoods where students most needed access at home. Internet-enabled school buses allow students access to be connected on the bus and in their own neighborhoods (McCrea, 2015).

NEW DIRECTIONS FOR STUDENT LEADERSHIP • DOI: 10.1002/yd

The third digital citizenship element in the respect category is *digital law*, "the electronic responsibility for actions and deeds" (Ribble, 2015, p. 42). Digital law includes the laws that govern Internet activities, that is, digital copyright, software pirating, stealing online identities, Internet scams, hacks, and so on (Bearden, 2016). For example, students introduced to the elements of digital law will know how to properly search and cite images, sources, and music using proper copyright, as well as issues surrounding the sharing of inappropriate images like sexting (i.e., the taking and sharing of sexually explicit images), which have criminal charges associated with both the person sending and receiving the images (Ribble, 2015).

Educate Yourself and Others.   The words of futurist Alvin Toffler (1970) are just as relevant today and can easily be applied to digital citizenship: "The illiterate of the 21st century will not be those who cannot read and write, but those who cannot learn, unlearn, and relearn" (p. 414). With the speed of changing technologies and their impact on society, the concept of lifelong learning becomes even more important. The skills of online and digital life are changing so rapidly that we are seeing microgenerational shifts where children born only a few years apart have a different experience with the technology (Anderson & Raine, 2012). Because the landscape of social media is constantly being updated with new and improved applications and tools, what tools students are currently using can change rapidly and in a relatively short amount of time; students will experience a new variety of digital tools throughout their educational career.

The three digital citizenship elements that fit within the theme of educate are literacy, communication, and commerce. *Digital literacy* specifically relates to digital citizenship by encompassing life skills that focus on finding, using, summarizing, evaluating, creating, and communicating information while using a variety of digital technologies (Ribble, 2015). Paul Gilster, author of *Digital Literacy* (1997), defined digital literacy as "the ability to understand information and—more important—to evaluate and integrate information in multiple formats . . . being able to evaluate and interpret information is critical" (p. 6). To be a socially responsible digital citizen, students need to learn how to navigate online learning networks and platforms; evaluate online resources; and understand digital basics such as browsers, search engines, email, and other digital literacy tools. Instead of asking our students to hand in work to the teacher, students need to be encouraged to publish their work on online platforms for an authentic audience while putting digital literacy into action.

The second digital citizenship element in the educate category is *communication,* which helps connect people across the room as well as around the world. It is important to focus on the message first, then decide which method (e.g., email, Twitter, and Facebook) may be the best to get the idea across. Understanding the tools, then considering the methods available will provide the best option for students to effectively communicate with a global audience.

The third digital citizenship element in the educate category is *digital commerce,* which provides an open marketplace not only in the community but across the globe. Students must understand when buying and selling online, much personal information is shared to complete these transactions. Students need to be aware of how best to protect their personal information while still having the ability to access to these opportunities. Students also need to understand there are costs associated with buying items online and that these are not free at the click of a button (Ribble, 2015).

Protect Yourself and Others.   Protection covers the last of the core themes and continues the focus of thinking beyond oneself and considering others when online. The three digital citizenship elements that fit within the theme of protect are rights and responsibilities, security, and health and wellness. *Digital rights and responsibilities* focus on being good stewards both on and offline. The goal is to help students humanize the person next to them as well as the across the screen (Curran, 2012). Educators need to provide students opportunities to recognize the responsibility behind their actions as we embed digital citizenship elements into an existing curriculum.

For some parents, the issues surrounding digital rights and responsibilities include having access to students' passwords, or having ability to see accounts on social networking sites. As a parent, this is not an invasion of privacy; instead, it is a way to better know your child, view how they interact with others, and keep them safe. Parents are responsible for their children and respect must be earned on both sides. For example, social cruelty affects everyone involved including the aggressor, target, and witnesses or bystanders. Providing opportunities for students to transform from "bystanders" to "upstanders" is true digital citizenship as it helps students build digital and social literacy in relationship to digital rights and responsibilities. Making this switch from bystander to upstander enables students to recognize their rights and responsibilities.

The second digital citizenship element in the protect category is *digital security,* which is both the protection of digital information as well providing safekeeping for others. Often personal data are shared online without fully understanding the consequences of an unintended audience. Without digital citizenship being embedded into the curriculum, students are not fully educated nor protected when they do not know about privacy settings (boyd, 2014). In today's connected world, security is the responsibility of everyone (Ribble, 2015).

The third digital citizenship element in the protect category is *digital health and wellness.* This category needs to be modeled and practiced on a daily basis by students and the adults in their lives. Finding a balance between one's online lives and the real world is a challenge. Research is finding that many technology users are addicted to their technology (Chait, 2013; Common Sense Media, 2016). The tools of technology are helping us to monitor and push us to increased health, but we must also put down technology to meet these needs. For some there are fears of not keeping up with others (FOMO—Fear of Missing Out) to such an extent that those who keep their phones near their beds interrupt their sleep patterns (Rettner, 2011).

Because students are coming to school with exposure to technology and social media, it is important that educators and parents are an integral part of the process of educating them about digital citizenship. To start this process, the first repetition focused on respect begins in kindergarten and continues through second grade (Common Sense Media, 2013). The topics of digital etiquette, digital communication, and digital rights and responsibilities would be integrated into the lessons throughout these grade levels. This does not preclude other skills or ideas from being taught, but it would provide a basis of creating skills-based lessons for this age of students. It would also begin to create a baseline of knowledge for all students at these class levels. When each repetition was complete, there would be a review of these skills to prepare the students to move on to repetition number two and another set of skills. Just like an athlete, the elements of repetition one are not forgotten but are built upon through repetitions two and three (Ribble, 2015).

A P–20 Digital Citizenship Curriculum

Using REP as a foundation for the P–20 model, students will be introduced to digital citizenship elements and themes that will continue to be reinforced and built upon starting with the youngest learners. Digital citizenship curriculum must start as soon as children begin using technology. Most likely this will start in the home, so parents must be included in the education process in order to be prepared on how to use technology responsibly. Even if the youngest learners do not have access to technology or handheld devices, they emulate the adults in their lives in many ways, so appropriate technology use, specifically tech balance, is critical (Meltzoff, 1999). The youngest learners are not necessarily predisposed to be technology users, but with little knowledge of potential issues they will begin to use as they have seen others do (Ribble, 2015). Adults model and teach about dangers and precautions in the physical world (such as a hot stove or traffic on the street) and these dangers and precautions need to be applied to digital and online choices (Common Sense Media, 2013; 2016).

The Early Years: Early and Often.   Instead of focusing on what to avoid, as well as the possible dangers and precautions, elementary teachers like Kayla Delzer are using the REP model to create authentic opportunities to model and teach digital citizenship (Delzer, 2015; 2016). Connected educators like Delzer are using classroom Twitter accounts to provide young students with an opportunity to practice positive social media use. Classroom Twitter accounts allow students to create and share with the world using a variety of digital tools like Skype or Google Hangout to connect to and collaborate with global classrooms. To further support this position, a third grader, Curran Dee, recently gave a TEDxYouth talk and shared, "If you want us to learn about the world, we have to learn with the world" (Dee, 2016). Breaking down classroom walls to connect through social media tools demonstrates social media is a powerful learning tool that allows students not to just read or write about digital citizenship. Students move from an awareness of being socially responsible to participatory citizenship to ultimately becoming justice-oriented citizens who address inequalities, uncover injustices, and work toward systematic solutions and change in local, global, and digital communities (Kahne, Chi, & Middaugh, 2006).

The Middle and High School Years. Just as identified in other skill areas, the coursework in the upper division classes would provide for an opportunity to truly explore how these tools might be used at a more complex level.

Connected educators like Jennifer Scheffer (2014; 2015a) provide real world learning opportunities to apply higher level thinking specifically in digital citizenship. Scheffer runs the Burlington High School Help Desk where students actively engage with modeling positive and practical use of social media and technology. Her curriculum helps students establish positive e-reputations through (1) the creation of digital resumes (e.g., LinkedIn, About.Me), (2) use of social media tools like Twitter and Snapchat as educational tools, and (3) the creation of websites, blogs, and digital portfolios to enhance their online presence (Scheffer, 2014). If curriculum included a REP model, students in courses like the Help Desk would be focused on best practices both in and out of the classroom:

> Many schools nationwide are still denying students (and teachers for that matter) access to the real-world digital citizenship learning opportunities. This outdated strategy leaves students unprepared for the digital future...However, when schools encourage safe, ethical, and savvy use of technology, and empower teachers to integrate technology into the curriculum, they are making a commitment to do what's right for digital natives. (Scheffer, 2015b, para. 11)

One of Scheffer's high school seniors, Timmy Sullivan, recently presented at the inaugural Digital Citizenship Summit in October 2015 and shared both personal anecdotes and professional sources challenging the myth of students being "digital natives," while demonstrating the need for digital citizenship embedded into curriculum and instruction. In a reflective blog post after the conference, he shared how digital citizenship curriculum not only prevents cyberbullying but also helps produce college- and career-ready students (Sullivan, 2015).

Implementing Digital Citizenship in Colleges and Universities. Digital citizenship has gained traction and momentum with K–12 educators but is relatively a new concept in higher education (Ahlquist, 2016;

Curran, 2012). Because many college students are legally able to vote, it is crucial that the focus is on being an active citizen both on and offline, in local, global, as well as digital communities is embedded into the curriculum (Ahlquist, 2016; Bearden, 2016; Curran, 2012; Ribble, 2015).

As stated earlier, the three types of digital citizens—personally responsible, participatory, and justice oriented—can all be experienced through a project-based learning (PBL) model (Kahne, Chi, & Middaugh, 2006). In the fall of 2011, incoming freshmen enrolled in a first-year seminar, *Pleased to Tweet You: Are You a Socially Responsible Digital Citizen?*, were expecting the course to promote consciousness and empathy online, but as the semester evolved, so did the course. The collaborative project connected the college freshmen in West Hartford, Connecticut with high school juniors in Birmingham, Alabama through social media tools like Twitter and Skype. What started as a way to create socially responsible digital citizens became an opportunity for the students to become actively involved in social justice issues in local, global, and digital communities. The final collaborative multimedia project became more than just a school project; it was a transformative experience for both the college freshmen and high school juniors as they became focused on changing minds, attitudes, and hearts.

The iCitizen Project defined by Curran (2012) reveals a new heuristic lens that expands digital citizenship to include an interconnected, local, global, and digital perspective. Curran defined an iCitizen as being aware, empathetic, socially responsible, and action oriented in regard to social justice issues. Curran's study revealed the students' definition of an iCitizen as a citizen of the world:

> An iCitizen is someone who is a citizen of the world. An iCitizen does not disconnect themselves from the other 195 nations. Instead, he sees these nations as his home and therefore sticks up for others regardless of national, cultural, political similarities. An iCitizen sees every person as a human first. If we are all human, don't we all deserve the same treatment? Be a person who has dignity for themselves and the world, be an iCitizen. (p. 10)

Despite the fact that the college seminar ended in December and final grades had been posted, the college freshmen and high school juniors did not want the iCitizen Project to end. During the spring semester, both classes co-moderated a #digcit chat in January 2012. The defining moment during the chat was witnessing the power of student voice and ownership. Tweets during the chat revealed the transformation. For example, Justice Wallace tweeted, "@mbfxc the #iCitizenProject was an amazing experience for me, because it really opened my eyes to something bigger than all of us. #digcit" (Wallace, 2012). Natasha Tripp added to this sentiment and tweeted, "@mbfxc @MsSandersTHS being able to skype w/ different students from another state & creating something so big & hving so many other ppl involved" (Tripp, 2012). What started as collaborative PBL assignment became an opportunity for students to model digital leadership with a global audience. Educators also joined the student-led chat and were interacting with the student moderators. The students were no longer just studying digital citizenship, they were actively applying being digital citizens or as they coined it, iCitizens.

The collaborative iCitizen Project (Curran, 2012) and the student-led digital citizenship chat on Twitter supports the fact that when students are actively engaged, the learning is authentic and meaningful. This was evident in the students' words and actions as they demonstrated a local, global, and digital understanding. The following month, Curran planned an iCitizenship town hall meeting on campus. The event included a live and virtual audience and the students once again took the lead. The 2-hour town hall event was livestreamed and live tweeted for a virtual audience resulting in over 800 tweets. The livestream was watched across the country and around the world. In fact, the countries Australia, Canada, and Jordan were recorded as viewers of the livestream. The iCitizen Project provided the basis for the following implications and conclusions:

1. Engaging K–12 and college students in iCitizenship is essential for 21st-century learners;
2. Empathy must be modeled and taught early and often;
3. Learning is social. Social media must be a part of K–12 and college curriculum and instruction;
4. Student-focused PBL is important in K–12 and college classrooms; and
5. Learning is a two-way street: teachers and students need to model being both learners and teachers in the classroom. (Curran, 2012)

A Community Approach: It Takes a Village

According to Hollandsworth, Dowdy, and Donovan (2011), it takes a village to teach digital citizenship. "Students use technology at home before they start school, requiring parents to begin teaching their children digital citizenship as soon as they begin to use a computer" (p. 40). Clark was quoted in Hollandsworth, Dowdy, and Donovan's research stating: "If we don't take the lead on this issue, they (students) will take the lead. We cannot afford to assume this won't happen. Teachers set the tone and need to be advocates of digital citizenship" (p. 42).

Embedding digital citizenship both on and offline and in and out of school is essential in making the nine digital citizenship elements part of our personal and professional lives. Courses like the Student Help Desk will prepare students to apply digital citizenship through real-world, authentic learning experiences that benefit both the students and the broader school community. If schools can be educational hubs then what happens in the classroom will happen outside of the classroom (Bearden, 2016). Using social media as a learning tool to solve problems changes the culture of a community. The key to the REP model is to have students, educators, parents, and the community members actively practice digital citizenship (Bearden, 2016; Curran, 2012; Hollandsworth et al., 2011; Ribble, 2015; Scheffer, 2015).

Recommendations for P–20 Educational Leaders

In an age where communication can be done instantly, being able to understand and navigate the World Wide Web as a socially aware, responsible, and justice-oriented digital citizen is imperative. Understanding, modeling, and engaging P–20 students in this critical conversation is the key to addressing the range of problems associated with not including digital citizenship into K–12 curriculum and instruction. Digital citizenship cannot be taught in isolation and needs to be experienced. Our teens are constantly being challenged to balance face-to-face and online relationships. Technology has changed the landscape of education, so educators (at all levels) must become proficient with the use of the technology to the extent of how it is to be integrated into the curriculum. These opportunities provide both teacher and student the ability to explore the opportunities that digital citizenship provides to help positively change communities locally, globally, and digitally.

References

Ahlquist, J. (2016, January 6). Infusing digital citizenship into higher education. LinkedIn [Web log comment]. Retrieved from https://www.linkedin.com/pulse/infusing-digital-citizenship-higher-education-dr-josie-ahlquist

Anderson, J. & Raine, L. (2012, February 29). Main findings: Teens, technology, and human potential in 2020. Pew Research Center. Retrieved from http://www.pewinternet.org/2012/02/29/main-findings-teens-technology-and-human-potential-in-2020/

Bearden, S. (2016). Digital citizenship: A community-based approach. Thousand Oaks, CA: Corwin.

boyd, d. (2014). It's complicated: The social lives of networked teens. New Haven, CT: Yale University Press.

Common Sense Media. (2013). Zero to eight: Children's media use in America. Retrieved from https://www.commonsensemedia.org/research/zero-to-eight-childrens-media-use-in-america-2013

Common Sense Media. (2016). Technology addiction: Concerns, controversy and finding balance. Retrieved from https://www.commonsensemedia.org/sites/default/files/uploads/research/csm_2016_technology_addiction_research_brief_0.pdf

Chait, J. (2013, July 21). Technology and kids: Startling statistics every parent should know about addiction to iPhones and screens [Web log comment]. Retrieved from http://www.inhabitots.com/technology-and-kids-startling-statistics-about-addiction-to-iphones-screens-that-every-parent-should-know/

Curran, M. B. F. X. (2012). iCitizen: Are you a socially responsible digital citizen? Paper presented at the International Society for Technology in Education's annual conference, San Diego, CA. Retrieved from http://www.isteconference.org/2012/program/search_results_details.php?sessionid=70224475

Dee, C. (2016, January 26). Speaking at the #DigCitSummitUK [Web log comment]. Retrieved from http://aroundtheworldwithcurran.blogspot.com/2016/01/speaking-at-digcitsummituk.html

Delzer, K. (2015, June 25). How you can become a champion of digital citizenship in your classroom. EdSurge [Web log comment]. Retrieved from https://www.edsurge.com/news/2015-06-25-how-you-can-become-a-champion-of-digital-citizenship-in-your-classroom

Delzer, K. (2016, February 3). Three reasons students should own your classroom's Twitter and Instagram accounts. EdSurge [Web log comment]. Retrieved from https://www.edsurge.com/news/2016-02-03-three-reasons-students-should-own-your-classroom-s-twitter-and-instagram-accounts

Douglas, T. (2014). Citizenship—digital and otherwise: The responsibility lies with our students and ourselves. entsekt, 1(2), 28–32.

Hollandsworth, R., Dowdy, L., & Donovan, J. (2011). Digital citizenship in K–12: It takes a village. Tech Trends: Linking Research & Practice to Improve Learning, 55, 37–47.

Gilster, P. (1997). Digital Literacy. New York, NY: John Wiley & Sons Inc.

Kahne, J., Chi, B., & Middaugh, E. (2006). Building social capital for civic and political engagement: The potential of high-school civics courses. Canadian Journal of Education, 29(2), 387–409.

Kang, C. (2016, February 22). Bridging a digital divide that leaves schoolchildren behind. New York Times [Web log comment]. Retrieved from http://www.nytimes.com/2016/02/23/technology/fcc-internet-access-school.html?_r=1

Meltzoff, A. N. (1999). Born to learn: What infants learn from watching us. In N. Fox & J. G. Worhol (Eds.), The role of early experience in infant development. Skillman, NJ: Pediatric Institute Publications. Retrieved from http://ilabs.washington.edu/meltzoff/pdf/99Meltzoff_BornToLearn.pdf

McCrea, B. (2015, April 30). WiFi on wheels puts two districts on the fast track to 24/7 access. THE Journal. Retrieved from https://thejournal.com/articles/2015/04/30/wifi-on-wheels.aspx

Ohler, J. (2016). 4Four big ideas for the future: Understanding our innovative selves. Anchorage, AK: CreateSpace Independent Publishing Platform.

Rettner, R. (2011). Nighttime gadget use of interferes with young adults health. Retrieved from http://www.livescience.com/35536-technology-sleep-adolescents.html

Ribble, M. (2011). Digital citizenship in schools (2nd ed.). Portland, OR: International Society for Technology in Education.

Ribble, M. (2015). Digital citizenship in schools (3rd ed.). Portland, OR: International Society for Technology in Education.

Scheffer, J. (2014, January 1). Ideas for teaching digital citizenship in 2014 [Web log comment]. Retrieved from https://jennscheffer.wordpress.com/2014/01/01/ideas-for-teaching-digital-citizenship-in-2014/

Scheffer, J. (2015, October 8). Let's get real: Reflections on the first national digital citizenship summit [Web log comment]. Retrieved from https://jennscheffer.wordpress.com/2015/10/08/lets-get-real-reflections-on-the-first-national-digital-citizenship-summit/

Scheffer, J. (2015a, January 11). Going global with Google hangouts [Web log post]. Retrieved from https://jennscheffer.wordpress.com/2015/01/11/going-global-with-google-hangouts/

Scheffer, J. (2015b, October 8). Let's get real: Reflections on the first national digital citizenship summit [Web log comment]. Retrieved from https://jennscheffer.

wordpress.com/2015/10/08/lets-get-real-reflections-on-the-first-national-digital-citizenship-summit/

Sullivan, T. (2015, October 4). Digital citizenship best practices for college and career ready students [Web log comment]. Retrieved from https://timmysullivan.com/2015/10/04/digitalcitizenship/

Toffler, A. (1970). Future shock. New York, NY: Random House.

Tripp, N. [ntripp_THStweet]. (2012, January, 11). @mbfxc @MsSandersTHS being able to skype w/ diff. students from another state &creating something so big &hving so many other ppl involved [Tweet]. Retrieved from https://twitter.com/TiaraTtweets/status/157262010323697664

Wallace, J. [Justicewwallace]. (2012, January, 11). @mbfxc the #iCitizenProject was an amazing experience for me because it really opened my eyes to something bigger than all of us. #digcit [Tweet]. Retrieved from https://twitter.com/Justice-wwallace/status/157262073460555777

MARIALICE B. F. X CURRAN is a connected educator specializing in digital citizenship in K–12 education, higher education, and teacher education and is the founder and chief executive officer of the Digital Citizenship Institute.

MIKE RIBBLE is the author of Digital Citizenship in Schools (3rd ed.), and has written and spoken on the topic both within the United States and internationally. He is also a founding member of the Digital Citizenship Institute and past cochair of the ISTE Digital Citizenship PLN.

NEW DIRECTIONS FOR STUDENT LEADERSHIP • DOI: 10.1002/yd

Social media tools are ubiquitous throughout the college student experience, particularly for students who hold leadership positions on campus. A research study on junior and senior student leaders' social media use and experience led to a number of findings that inform leadership education practice.

Digital Student Leadership Development

Josie Ahlquist

"I have always been told what not to do online. But no one has ever told me what I'm supposed to do on social media."
 -Senior student leader, research participant at a large public institution

On college and university campuses, educators invest time, resources, and even pride in student leaders. These students take on positions of power and influence, from student government president to resident assistant, delivering student services to their peers and ideally making an impact on the entire university community. Because student leaders have grown up with social media communication tools and have had daily interactions with technology, they bring a wealth of existing experience and perspective to their positions. However, these digital experiences have not been formally studied nor are they understood in leadership education. As a result, adults have maintained largely unfavorable views of the use of technology by youth (boyd, 2014; Junco, 2014), and this has led to restrictive social media policies and negative education models).

As noted in the opening quotation from a very involved college student, the only message usually delivered by family, campus supervisors, and society is what not to do on social media. This chapter aims to serve this student and thousands of others by demonstrating what is possible on social media when viewed through the lens of leadership. It answers the question, What does successful student leadership look like in our digital age? This chapter opens by relating the background of leadership and social media used by youth, then it features the results of a study that explored the experiences and use of social media by 40 college student leaders. Finally, curriculum for

NEW DIRECTIONS FOR STUDENT LEADERSHIP, no. 153, Spring 2017 © 2017 Wiley Periodicals, Inc., A Wiley Company
Published online in Wiley Online Library (wileyonlinelibrary.com) • DOI: 10.1002/yd.20229

digital student leadership development and the role of leadership educators online are proposed.

Students' Attraction to Social Media

A variety of social media applications have been available since the early 2000s. Myspace came out in 2003, Facebook was released in 2004, and the first video was uploaded to YouTube in 2005. Therefore, by 2017, college students such as the Class of 2020 could have been using social media tools since elementary school. Concerns exist that over this time online communication has been replacing face-to-face communication; however, Huang, Hood, and Yoo (2013) documented that this access facilitates offline interaction and does not replace it. In Sponcil and Gitimu's (2013) study on social media use by college students, face-to-face interaction was actually found to be preferred over Internet-aided communication.

danah boyd (2014) gave insight into youths' intent in using social media. She uses the term "networked publics," which she defines as:

> publics that are restructured by networked technologies. As such, they are simultaneously (1) the space constructed through networked technologies and (2) the imagined community that emerges as a result of the intersection of people, technology, and practice (p. 5).

In her study, boyd found that teens overwhelmingly sought out networked publics for relationships with their peers, even though fearful parents and teachers used many conflicting and confrontational tactics to dissuade them. Challenging society's perceptions, what boyd calls "fear mongering," was behind why youth were drawn to or actually active on social media tools (2014 p. 26). She further described fear mongering thus: "Teens are both public menaces and vulnerable targets. Society is afraid of them and for them. The tension between these two views shapes adults' relationship with teens and our societal beliefs about what it is that teenagers do" (2014 p. 160). Unfortunately, boyd's description of parents' perceptions of social media might also fit those of some higher education administrators at some institutions.

A prominent researcher on social media in higher education, Rey Junco (2014) defined society's negative view of social media as an adult normative perspective, "what is appropriate based upon their [adults] own expectations and norms; these expectations are no doubt influenced by popular media portrayals of social media as detrimental to youth development" (p. 96). Therefore, their perspective is not based on what youth are actually doing on social media but on worst-case scenarios. This same adult normative perspective may be prevalent among higher education administrators at some institutions. However, as both boyd (2014) and Junco (2014) have found, there are differences between what society fears youth are using social media for, and the reality of what is truly going on.

Viewing leadership through the lens of technology tools requires knowledge and understanding of actual social media use by teens and young adults, who are typically the most frequent users of these tools. In 2015, the most popular platform was Facebook, with research finding 90–99% of college students logging on daily (Chen & Marcus, 2012). This frequent usage was also a major finding in the 2015 Pew Research Center *Americans' Internet Access* report, which documents that 96% of youth from ages 18 to 29 use the Internet (Perrin & Duggan, 2015). Other recent research has shown that youth are not just using social media tools daily, but multiple times a day (Ellison, Steinfield, & Lampe, 2007).

Youth born after 1980 have been labeled "digital natives" because they have grown up with digital technology (Prensky, 2001). They now arrive on college campuses equipped with devices such as laptops, smartphones, and tablets that offer constant connection. Although students have been exposed to digital tools since birth, they are not always fully literate or competent in their use. Instead, they face a disconnection caused by the absence of digital literacy education in their schools' curricula. This is compounded by the fact that in our networked age, new invention, innovation, disruption, and discovery occur continuously. Technology continues to emerge, remix, and evolve, and the education field struggles to keep up. As higher education practitioners explore ways to develop student leaders, their technology use, especially social media, must be considered.

Leadership in the Digital Age

Over time, there has been a change in perspective regarding college student leadership from leader centric, in which a student needs a position to be a leader, to collaboration centric, in which anyone can develop leadership ability (Komives & Dugan, 2010) and engage in the leadership process with others. In addition, contemporary theories of leadership prioritize self-awareness, ethics, morality, and social responsibility. This shift is reflected in the four major leadership theories that are popular in college student leadership research and programmatic application: transformational leadership (Bass, 1985), emotional intelligence leadership (Shankman, Allen, & Haber-Curran, 2015), relational leadership (Komives, Lucas, & McMahon, 2013), and the social change model of leadership development (Higher Education Research Institute [HERI], 1996). The latter three models charge leaders to be change agents, aware of self and committed to others in working toward a common purpose and positive change.

This chapter aims to show how the social change model (HERI, 1996), specifically, can be used to develop digital student leaders. Individual, group, and community values ground this leadership development model to aid college students in becoming agents for positive social change. There are seven values including (individual level) consciousness of self, congruence, commitment; (group level) common purpose, collaboration, controversy with civility; and (community level) citizenship (HERI, 1996; Komives & Dugan, 2010). How these seven values interact contributes to socially responsible leadership. So what would this leadership look like on an application like Facebook or Instagram?

LaRiviere, Snider, Stromberg, and O'Meara (2012) connected student social activism and digital media to positive social change. The authors demonstrate that because the Internet allows for various points of connection, student activists have opportunities to jump over hierarchical leadership structures to make change happen. LaRiviere et al. (2012) state: "Educators have a responsibility to help students wield social media as a tool that educates, strengthens commitments, and contributes to social change" (p. 16). Therefore, digital technology education should not be merely the introduction of tools; rather, it should guide students on ways to effectively take advantage of social media in their roles on campus, as active members of the global community, and as future leaders in their chosen professions.

Researching the College Student Leader Digital Experience

To understand digital leadership and provide educational tools for leadership development, I conducted a yearlong study that explored student leaders' perceptions of social media and the meaning they make of digital technologies in their college experience. The study specifically focused on the ways student leaders made digital decisions through the lenses of identity and leadership through a mixed methods sequential exploratory design (Tashakkori & Teddlie, 1998). I identified participants through purposeful sampling, seeking out 40 junior and senior university student leaders. The study defined a student leader as a college student who was involved in a traditional student leader role for which he or she was selected, nominated, hired, or elected. Participants were nominated by higher education professionals on each campus who could confirm they met the study's requirements: (a) good standing in a student leadership position, (b) at least 1 year of experience in a leadership-related campus position, and (c) active accounts on at least two social media platforms.

Research was conducted over three distinct phases. First, I administered six 90-minute focus groups and collected 40 responses to a questionnaire. I analyzed focus group data through qualitative techniques and online questionnaire data through descriptive statistics. Then, using the results from this phase, I developed an instrument in the form of a social media rubric for the second, quantitative phase. This rubric included behaviors seen in posts, specifically values of the social change model in social media activity. I focused on Facebook and Instagram because participants reported these two platforms were the ones they most actively used. I quantitized (Teddlie & Tashakkori, 2009) 2,200 qualitative social media posts for statistical analysis, using numeric values from my social media rubric to code the data set and administer statistical analysis. Finally, I merged data from phases one and two to provide a thick description in phase three through a matrix.

As a result, the research produced five major findings: (a) social media impact starting in K–12, (b) college student leaders' use of social media, (c) presentation of digital identity, (d) leadership presence and possibilities, and (e) significance of social media guidance (Ahlquist, 2015). Four of these findings are expanded in the rest of the chapter, providing a direct line from research to practice.

The Digital Timeline of Today's College Student Leaders

Especially in the focus groups, social media stories from student leader participants surfaced in unexpected ways. This included reflection on what it felt like to first get onto an online social platform, struggling with conflict between family members on Facebook, and the fishbowl effect they felt everyday on campus and online now that they were student leaders.

Scrolling Through K–12 Online History.   College student leaders' social media use and experience was not isolated to their time in college. Rather, it began in middle school, and in the focus groups, participants shared that it was during these years they experienced the majority of regret, such as posting something negative about family members or stumbling onto a chatroom where they felt uncomfortable. Heads nodded in unison when embarrassing stories about childish decisions made on Myspace or Facebook were shared. By high school, the participants began to receive guidance from family and peers and at school. Thus, both researchers and practitioners need to look holistically at how these tools have been part of students' lives over time. Especially in the focus groups, the participants unpacked early teen adoption and tied it back to current perspectives on social media.

The College Student Leader Digital Experience.   After analyzing posts on the top use sites of Facebook and Instagram, I noted they were used primarily for posting visual content with the intention of sharing relationships and expressing interests. This included photos of self, groups, and objects or scenery. Participants also used social media to interact with each other by making comments, sharing their interests, and posting about their leadership positions. A few examples of posts related to leadership positions included group photos with other leaders (e.g., resident assistants), campus events, or promoting a program. I discovered this finding in both phases one and two of the study, as during the focus groups, participants expressed a desire to maintain relationships and self-expression through social media. Unlike Instagram, Facebook activity appeared to be slightly different, with less personal activity but more in-depth expression, such as including photos, text, and tags all in one post. Using a mixed methodology, study allowed me to capture a complete understanding of usage including both self-reported data and actual usage. Mixing these data showed that

NEW DIRECTIONS FOR STUDENT LEADERSHIP • DOI: 10.1002/yd

participants were likely posting more about themselves than they realized and showed conflicting social media perspectives on what their role is in presenting social change.

What I also captured throughout the phases of research was that participants in the focus groups were confident, they were posting appropriately online and this was confirmed after I observed and analyzed their posts. I tested a scale of appropriateness, rating posts as appropriate, blurry, or inappropriate when exploring professional decision making on social media. More than 97.5% of posts I labeled as appropriate and further observed activity that displayed open reflection. There were, however, discrepancies in appropriate usage, which emerged during the phase two statistical analysis through positional and demographic differences in blurry and inappropriate posts. A post would be categorized as "blurry" if the post could possibly be viewed as conflicting or even confusing to a third party. An example of this classification included a student who was 21, yet the majority of their posts were alcohol related. Although legally appropriate, the pattern of behavior became conflicting with their leadership position. Examples of inappropriate posts included harsh language, excessive intake of alcohol, inappropriate attire, and drug use. When comparing all student leader positions, Greek life student leaders were more likely to post inappropriate or blurry, conflicting content. However, at the same time, the same Greek student leaders were more likely to display a number of values of the social change model. A number of these behaviors included volunteering, civil discourse in comments, mentoring new students, and active reflection in their posts. I advocate all of these actions in digital leadership education for college students. So how do we teach Greek affiliated students to have a stronger balance? Some of this was discovered back in the focus groups.

The opportunity for participants to explain themselves honors their experiences and can aid educators in connecting digital behavior with leadership skills. Based upon the methodology of this study, students voiced their stories in the focus groups and I developed questions to ask during those groups that allowed participants to explore their experiences with social media over time. These experiences began as early as elementary school and continued into the positive and negative realities of social media use in college. Stories about the participants' experiences in college were fueled with more emotions, which many times included frustration. Students related that they approached controversy, conflict, and confusion daily as they logged onto social media applications. Even so, they were even more drawn to them, finding connections and maintaining relationships. Online activity was successfully conducted by student leaders by using a basic, internal reflective checklist that aided in making decisions, which included asking themselves questions like "Is this appropriate?," "Would my grandma approve?," and/or "Do I look good?"

Participants described the serious weight of their leadership positions, which affected how they expressed themselves on social media. They talked about leadership contracts, campus responsibilities, and supervisor expectations. This sometimes had a silencing impact on their true self. In the focus groups, participants explained the deeper impact of this silence, which describes why the participants chose not to participate in digital expressions of social justice or community service, commonly referred to as "social media for social good." The participants described the efforts to which they went not to post anything controversial and described their role as student leaders was to be politically correct and not pick sides. This played out on Facebook and Instagram, where posts were less likely to contain content that represented group and community values from the social change model.

Discovering Digital Leadership Skills.   The primary focus of this study was on student leadership in the digital age. By selecting participants holding leadership positions and building a research framework using the social change model, I was able to explore what leadership looked like on social media. As a result, I discovered leadership presence and leadership-like behavior both was and was not presented by the participants online. After applying a social media rubric to online activity, I found the individual values of the social change model were the highest presented. This included the expression of consciousness of self and commitment. Although some guidance was provided to the participants, I found they mostly learned digital skills on their own over time through trial and error, which led to these values being presented. However, individual values are only one part of the social change model. The participants did not demonstrate group and community values through their online activity.

Significance of Social Media Guidance.   Through this research I discovered the importance and impact of digital education, confirming why 97.5% of the 2,200 social media posts by the participants were appropriate. Some students in specific positions were more likely to do this successfully than others, including student government-related positions and peer mentorships, because these students wanted to share leadership-related experiences with their digital communities. Investigating this result further, I discovered that where a student leader obtained previous social media guidance mattered. Guidance from K–12 institutions had a statistically significant negative impact on their positive usage of social media as college students. However, I also found that participants who received any kind of training or education during college were statistically more likely not only to post more appropriately but also to share more content related to the social change model (HERI, 1996). Other positive guidance influences included parents and peers.

Secret Sauce of Digital Education.   Results on previous digital education were further explained when I factored in two other questions asked in the social media questionnaire. First, whether participants had ever regretted a past social media post was positively related to current appropriate activity. This meant that student leaders who admitted they once regretted a post were more likely to post appropriately in the present. I also observed this reflective skill set when I monitored social media activity on Facebook and Instagram, where participants expressed self and others through posts on life events, celebrations, and journaling-like activities.

More substance for these two findings can be understood by returning to the focus groups, during which participants described how they made digital decisions. They related that how others would view the post was important to them. Students also considered privacy, as well as whether the post would represent how they wanted to be presented. Because of the positive outcome of their observed social media activity, I found the digital decision-making model they described in the focus group produced productive results.

The focus groups also provided information on how important relationships played out in social media activity, as well as the communities to which the student leaders felt responsible. This included their leadership positions, their universities and students, their families, and even future generations. These levels of responsibility played into the model the student leaders created to reflect on their digital activity. Mindfulness of social media communities and how they had an impact on them fueled their social media use. The results confirm the positive impact of digital education in college, especially on student leaders, and inform tools such as a reflective digital checklist, which all students could adopt as part of their posting practice. Additional implications were discovered in this research, which are featured in the five pillars of digital leadership education.

Pillars of Digital Leadership Education

The education of the whole person is a common component of many university mission statements, and it includes preparing students to become future leaders in the ever-changing world. However, research has shown an

Figure 4.1.   Digital Leadership Education Pillars

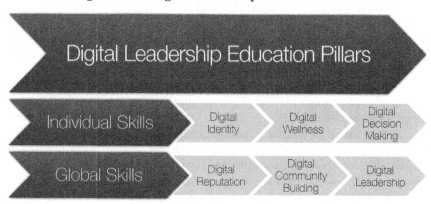

Figure 4.2.   Defining Digital Student Leadership

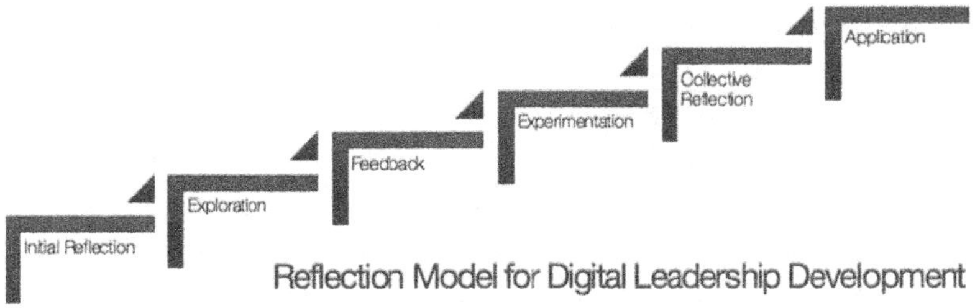

Reflection Model for Digital Leadership Development

important piece is largely missing from the curricula: education related to technology that influences and interacts constantly with student leadership practices, identity formation, and decision making. To fill this gap, I created a digital leadership curriculum that includes six pillars, which are the major, pivotal topics in the formation of digital student leaders in higher education settings. Showcased in Figure 4.1, they include digital identity, wellness, decision making, branding, community building, and leadership, all of which fall under either individual or global skills. Although education can start anywhere among the pillars, the individual-level topics lay a solid foundation for the development of leadership skills in the digital age. This model also lends itself to using the social change model as a framework within digital leadership education.

All of the pillars are surrounded by a digital reflection model, seen in Figure 4.2. The digital reflection model is a tool that can be used by leadership educators to create intentional curricula built around critical thinking and reflection on social media. This model is conceptualized from Kolb's experiential learning theory (1984). Kolb described learning in a four-stage cycle, "a concrete experience (CE), feeling dimension; reflective observation (RO), a watching dimension; abstract conceptualization (AC), a thinking dimension; and active experimentation (AE), a doing dimension" (Kolb, p. 38). This transformative process leads to knowledge and learning that uses reflection, experimentation, and action. As seen in my research results, students who reflected on their past behavior and used a reflective digital decision-making process were more likely to post productively in the present day. The reflection model for digital leadership development positions learners through reflection, exploration, feedback, experiment, collective, and application in each digital leadership education pillar.

Leadership that integrates technology is not to be confused with having the latest mobile applications or devices. Digital leaders are aware of, explore, and strategically implement innovative hardware and software technologies. Furthermore, digital leaders tap into the "heartware" of human relations on all communication platforms, both online and face to face, by plugging into communities and collaborating. They recognize the influence and impact they have on digital platforms, and their online actions should be congruent with their offline ones when meeting the same people. A digital student leader recognizes the power of social technology tools, including the effect of their online activity on their leadership capacity, and seeks out tools to better their community for positive social change. Building from the competencies of a digital student leader listed earlier in this chapter (Ahlquist, 2014), the pillars of digital leadership education intend to empower digital student leaders.

Digital Identity. Researcher Rey Junco (2014) defined digital identity as "the conscious or unconscious process by which people try to influence the perception of their image, typically through social interactions" (p. 111). Educating students on digital identities includes online self-awareness and reflection on their digital profile (Ahlquist, 2014). In the social change model (HERI, 1996), individual values (consciousness of self, congruence, and commitment) lend themselves to guiding students through the discernment and exploration of self both in traditional and virtual settings. Basic reflection questions include the following: Have you ever Googled yourself? Have you ever posted anything you later regretted? Why/why not? A more comprehensive digital identity assignment could include the following:

- Step 1: Google yourself and list the top 20 results. If nothing comes up with your name, also add in to the search the name of your hometown, college, or student organization. (Step 1a: Clean up anything that is false or negative.)
- Step 2: Create an Excel document, listing every social media platform with which you have an account. Note any privacy settings. Answer what you enjoy or dislike about each platform. List out how often you use this account.
- Step 3: Taking an outsider's perspective of your pages, what are the themes of your posts? Do you complain or post praise for others? Do you post pictures from parties or engaging life adventures? Do you post memes or quotes that reflect your values or positions?
- Step 4: Receive feedback from two people you respect (e.g., supervisor, mentor, family member, and peer student leader) on what they see from your public digital activity.
- Step 5: Reflect and journal, answering the following questions: What is the perception you want to give people through your social media activity? Does your current activity reflect this? Will you change any settings, edit posts, or reconsider usage on specific platforms? What action will you take to better connect your values, personality, and passions into your digital presence?

Digital Wellness. As noted in Chapter 3 of this volume, digital citizenship is another arm of curriculum even for the youngest of users in elementary school. Ribble, Bailey, and Ross (2004) produced nine digital citizenship elements: digital etiquette, communication, access, literacy, commerce, law, rights and responsibilities, health and wellness, and digital security. One of the elements, digital health and wellness, is defined as "physical and psychological well-being in a digital technology world" (Ribble, 2011, p. 11). I took this one step further, calling for "establishing personal virtual boundaries, including privacy, time management, and overall wellness" (Ahlquist, 2014, p. 59). The awareness of technology use in one's daily life is one place to start reflecting on this pillar. When conducting leadership workshops on social media, I ask participants to reflect on two questions: What is the first thing you typically do when you wake up? What is the last thing you do before you go to bed? Time and time again, the answer has to do with checking their phones and starting to scroll through text messages, social media, and email.

Brown (2016) researched how college students' sense of self surfaced on social media. He discovered the attraction to "likes" in getting attention on applications like Instagram. However, as students move from external definitions of self to an internal sense of self on social media, they are "owning social media as opposed to being owned by it" (Brown, 2016, p. 221). Taking ownership of the choices we make online and their impact on our sense of self is part of the core of digital wellness.

Digital Decision Making.   This pillar digs into an intentional reflective process for students to strategize social media use. Most simply, what do you choose to share, why, when, and where? Despite the students in my research feeling conflicted about the negative aspects of social media, participants continued to pursue ways to stay engaged online. This was made possible in the internal and external processes they put in place—in other words, how they made decisions about what they would or would not post (Ahlquist, 2015). As a result, participants addressed a number of considerations before posting, including level of appropriateness, their families, their leadership position, and the platform that made up this overall checklist. One junior student leader shared, "I ask myself if this is appropriate, if my grandma would like it, and if there's alcohol in the background. And if I look good in it." In this case, even if she answered yes to everything but alcohol, she would not post it.

This pillar employs activities and actions that call upon students to reflect on why they post what they do. It also educates them on the impact their social media activity has on their campus, local, and global communities and provides a means to strategize future use, including "digital decision making strategies based in positive, authentic, and constructive activity" (Ahlquist, 2014, p. 59). This is especially a key area to apply the digital reflection model, including asking for feedback from peers and mentors to understand the impact of digital decisions and further refine future online actions.

Digital Branding.   In *What Happens on Campus Stays on YouTube*, Qualman (2015) declared digital reputation is an asset that needs to be preserved and stated the number one purpose of digital reputation is to brand yourself, which "puts the power of reputation management in your own hands by providing tools for a do-it-yourself digital reputation audit" (p. 125). This audit can be done individually, or a campus can formalize this process, as the State University of New York (SUNY) College at Oswego has done through its Digital Dirt Squad, coordinated by its Career Services office. The program's mission is to help students understand the importance of their digital reputation and online identity. The Digital Dirt Squad performs damage control in some cases, but more often, it assists students in finding ways to leverage the power of social media to further their career development. The director of SUNY Oswego's career services office, Gary Morris, shared that the program assists students' through campus presentations, one-on-one personalized appointments, and continued research and marketing of content for campus distribution. Morris stated, "Three years in the running, our Digital Dirt Squad has served to successfully move our students into a more professionally supportive online environment" (personal communication, April 2016).

Digital Community Building.   The digital landscape calls for leaders to have a new skill set. No longer can they flourish in face-to-face meetings or create teams within traditional, physical office spaces. Business meetings have gone global with technology tools like Zoom or Skype, and customer interaction is 24/7 with social media applications like Twitter. These real-time and potentially viral interactions require communication and collaboration skills unlike any most leadership educators have seen before. In Chapter 6, Endersby, Phelps, and Jenkins further explore leading virtual teams. Digital community building sets up students for success in taking the social change model group and community values into the digital space. Specifically considering the controversy over civility value, what are the most effective approaches to resolving conflict online? This pillar also addresses what Chapter 5 unpacks on social justice and activism online. Digital leadership education should provide resources on how to use social media for social good, what Gismondi and Osteen in chapter 5 call digitally aided movements.

Digital Leadership.   As shared earlier in this chapter, digital leadership focuses on the "heartware" of technology. In other words, it is the business of human relations through social communication tools for the betterment of self and others. This takes conversations about digital identity, reputation, and branding to a more significant, global, and even spiritual level. To get started, ask students the following questions: If you could go viral for one passion you have, what would it be? If everything you posted and contributed online was to live on beyond you, what would you want that collective message and impact to be? Qualman (2015) calls this "the digital stamp they want to leave on this world" (p. 187). This makes one's digital reputation one's digital purpose.

At Florida State University, I teach an online course called *Leadership in the Digital Age* that uses the framework of the social change model (HERI, 1996) and the digital leadership education pillars. To date, the more than 175 undergraduate students who have enrolled in the course have been asked to think about social media as more than selfies, Instagram likes, and LinkedIn profiles. The learning objectives for the course instead aim for students to:

- Conceptually be able to discuss the social change model.
- Explore questions such as who they are online, who they are as a leader, what they want to accomplish, what issues they are passionate about, how their social media and online activity impact their leadership capacity, and what their social media strategy is as a leader.
- Develop the digital skills necessary to be an effective leader in the digital age, including communication and writing skills on Twitter and LinkedIn, as well as employ a digital decision-making model.
- Apply leadership theory to practice to enhance leadership skills, experience, and knowledge both in person and online.

How can your existing leadership programs weave in any of these digital leadership education pillars? Do you use core leadership theories that already provide common language for the campus that can be applied in a digital context? Digital leadership education does not need to be a new line in the budget, week of programming, or keynote speaker. However, it does need to be intentional and should begin with blending into existing successful programs.

Trending Toward the Future

Taking the results of this research, there are three major recommendations I propose for leadership education that recognizes the influence of technology in leadership development. First is starting digital education early. Second, is being intentional on training educators to build a community around them. Finally, is shifting the paradigm of how we view youth making mistakes online, imagining how to use these errors as learning and reflection opportunities for growth, not just issues to deal with through the judicial process. These recommendations call upon administrators, parents, faculty, and peer student leaders to be part of digital leadership education.

Start Digital Education Interventions Early.   The student leaders in my study revealed that their digital experiences started in their early teens, but they had limited formal education at the time. They admitted it was here that they struggled the most, especially as their experiences related to privacy, peer pressure, and making mistakes online. Most social media sites require users to be at least 13; however, participants admitted to having joined them much earlier. Interventions exploring digital literacy skills, such as etiquette, privacy, and what it means to be a good digital citizen, should be established starting at the age of 12 at the latest. As a student moves into high school, curriculum should be expanded to include digital identity and the expression and presentation of self in the digital space. Tying digital activity to future plans to attend college should interact with developing LinkedIn, blogging, and portfolio skills. High school interventions should also expand to a community level, not only to local community but also to global digital citizenship expression. Throughout each phase of a student's precollege digital education, they need to be supported with tangible tools they can immediately apply.

Building a Community of Digital Educators. A major finding of the study was the positive impact a number of sources had on the student leaders who were now producing positive content. They included both guidance in college and guidance from parents and peers. Little significance came from being self-taught despite this effort being mentioned as the primary source for the participants' guidance since their early teen years. Guidance in elementary, middle, and high school carried little support and, in some cases, even had a negative impact on later posting behavior. Taking into consideration these results, I recommend a community of digital educators be drafted. They should be seen formally on campus, as well as within existing programming, such as new student orientation and fall leader training by professional staff. Career services and student leadership administrators can support the cause of digital educators, including the philosophy of education on social media tools for positive purposes. This curriculum should be timed according to the developmental needs of students, building content not only around the pillars of digital leadership, but also woven into existing leadership models and theories used on campus.

Peers were another positive source of guidance for the participants. Recognizing this impact, peers should also be empowered and trained formally or informally and informally on how to be a digital educator. For example, peers can teach content to both first-year students and student leaders. This was especially significant for group values of the social change model. The creation of a peer digital educator team would expand university services to include support for students in understanding digital possibilities and advising them on correcting a digital mistake.

Turning Digital Mistakes into Positive Possibilities. Digital education should be rooted in guiding students and the entire campus community on the possibilities of social media tools instead of relating worst-case scenarios and advice on what not to do. Participants described the fear tactics they had heard since middle school, which continue to be presented today by the media, and restrictive policies related to their positions. As a result, a major finding of the study was the silencing impact student leadership positions had on online activity. The participants did not feel like they could truly express themselves, and as a result, they posted less frequently on social media.

Another major finding was the positive impact regretting a previous social media post had on current behavior. This result gives permission to students, as well as digital educators, to understand that mistakes are going to happen in online life, and more importantly, to reflect on these experiences and learn from them. This perspective should also be incorporated into student support services such as student conduct. If students make errors on a digital application, this sanctioning experience should be used as an opportunity to educate them on digital identity and community, especially through reflective tools for long-term learning.

Conclusion

This chapter considers the whole experience students are having in the 21st century, which includes both their life on campus and online. Students come to college with a digital history that has not yet been acknowledged in leadership development programs or theories. As the most frequent users of many social media applications, they have been at the focus of society's negative view of these tools, which has also crept in student leader policies, trainings, and programming.

This chapter shares the results of a mixed methods study on digital student leadership and a model that was developed in response (the six pillars for digital leadership education), which recognizes the influence technology has had on current college students since middle school and empowers its use through the community building and leadership capacity. Technology tools will continue to evolve and become more woven into our lives. Digital student leadership takes these realities to a positive place. Students and educators need to understand and embrace technology tools like social media and craft a digital purpose capable of trending beyond what any 140-character Twitter post can share.

References

Ahlquist, J. (2014). Trending now: Digital leadership education using social media and the social change model. *Journal of Leadership Studies, 8*(1), 57–60.

Ahlquist, J. (2015). *Developing digital student leaders: A mixed methods study of student leadership, identity and decision making on social media* (Doctoral dissertation). Retrieved from ProQuest Dissertations and Theses. (Accession No. 3713711)

Bass, B. M. (1985). *Leadership and performance beyond expectations*. New York, NY: Free Press.

boyd, s. (2014). *It's complicated: The social lives of networked teens*. New Haven, CT: Yale University.

Brown, P. G. (2016). *College students, social media, digital identities, and the digitized self* (Doctoral dissertation). Chestnut Hill, MA: Boston College.

Chen, B., & Marcus, J. (2012). Students' self-presentation on Facebook: An examination of personality and self-construal factors. *Computers in Human Behavior, 28*, 2091–2099.

Ellison, N., Steinfield, C., & Lampe, C. (2007). The benefits of Facebook "friends": Social capital and the college students' use of online social network sites. *Journal of Computer-Mediated Communication, 12*, 1143–1168.

Higher Education Research Institute. (1996). *A social change model of leadership development: Guidebook ver. III.* College Park, MD: National Clearinghouse for Leadership Programs.

Huang, W. H. D., Hood, D. W., & Yoo, S. J. (2013). Gender divide and acceptance of collaborative Web 2.0 applications for learning in higher education. *Internet and Higher Education, 16*, 57–65.

Junco, R. (2014). *Engaging students through social media: Evidence-based practices for use in student affairs.* San Francisco, CA: Jossey-Bass.

Kolb, D. A. (1984). *Experiential learning: Experience as the source of learning and development.* Upper Saddle River, NJ: Prentice Hall.

Komives, S. R., & Dugan, J. P. (2010). Contemporary leadership theories. In R. Couto (Ed.), *Political and civic leadership* (pp. 111–120). Thousand Oaks, CA: Sage.

Komives, S. R., Lucas, N., & McMahon, T. R. (2013). *Exploring leadership: For college students who want to make a difference* (3rd ed.). San Francisco, CA: Jossey-Bass.

LaRiviere, K., Snider, J., Stromberg, A., & O'Meara, K. (2012). Protest: Critical lessons of using digital media for social change. *About Campus, 17*(3), 10–17.

Perrin, A., & Duggan, M. (2015, June 26). Americans' internet access: 2000–2015. *Pew Research Center.* Retrieved from http://www.pewinternet.org/2015/06/26/americans-internet-access-2000-2015/

Prensky, M. (2001). Digital natives, digital immigrants. *On the Horizon, 9*(5), 1–6.

Qualman, E. (2015). *What happens on campus stays on YouTube.* Cambridge, MA: Equalman Studios.

Ribble, M. S., Bailey, G. D., & Ross, T. W. (2004). Digital citizenship: Focus questions for implementation. *Learning and Leading with Technology, 32*(2), 12–15.

Ribble, M. (2011). *Digital citizenship in schools* (2nd ed.). Eugene, OR: International Society in Education.

Shankman, M., Allen, S., & Haber-Curran, P. (2015). *Emotionally intelligent leadership. A guide for students.* San Francisco, CA: Jossey-Bass.

Sponcil, M., & Gitimu, P. (2013). Use of social media by college students: Relationship to communication and self-concept. *Journal of Technology Research, 4*, 1–13.

Tashakkori, A., & Teddlie, C. (1998). *Mixed methodology: Combining qualitative and quantitative approaches.* Thousand Oaks, CA: Sage.

Teddlie, C., & Tashakkori, A. (2009). *Foundations of mixed methods research.* Thousand Oaks, CA: Sage.

JOSIE AHLQUIST is a research associate and instructor in the Florida State University Leadership Learning Research Center, producing scholarship and education on leadership in the digital age. She is also an independent digital leadership speaker, consultant, and author at www.josieahlquist.com.

NEW DIRECTIONS FOR STUDENT LEADERSHIP • DOI: 10.1002/yd

5

This chapter discusses the emergent use of digital technology to inspire, connect, and sustain student activism on campus. An overview of student activism, opportunities, and challenges of this technology, along with recent case studies and implications for practice, are presented.

Student Activism in the Technology Age

Adam Gismondi, Laura Osteen

"It's happening again— it's like when we were here! It's happening!" Quoting his friend who is a trustee at Cornell University, Harold Levy captures both the excitement and concern of administrators as student activism arises on campuses across the nation (Wong, 2015, p. 5). Although "students and activism have long gone hand in hand" (Rue, personal communication, February 6, 2016), the recent emergence of protests, sit-ins, hunger strikes, and lists of student demands can be distinguished from protests of the past. Current calls for change "are less identified with distant others and more closely aligned with students' lived experiences" (Rue, personal communication, February 6, 2016). In addition to the identity-based and campus-located focus, the zeitgeist of today's student activism is defined by the prevalent use and amplified impact of technology. Today's student activists are inspired, connected, and sustained through the power of social networking sites (Hernández, 2015; New, 2016; Wong, 2015). To better understand this phenomenon, this chapter examines characteristics, case studies, and lessons learned from three recent digitally aided student movements: Occupy Wall Street, the 2012 tuition protests in Quebec, and Black Lives Matter. The chapter closes with implications for practice in order to recognize student activism as a partnership opportunity between students and campus administrators to guide institutions toward becoming the equitable and just learning environments our mission statements describe.

Calling for equity and justice, student activists around the world are learning, motivating, and communicating their messages of and strategies for change through mobile and social media. Protesting inequality, racism, rape, and administrators' responses to all of these, students are leading mass demonstrations, lying down in the streets, walking out of classes, and closing campus administration buildings. These acts of student activism are

New Directions for Student Leadership, no. 153, Spring 2017 © 2017 Wiley Periodicals, Inc., A Wiley Company
Published online in Wiley Online Library (wileyonlinelibrary.com) • DOI: 10.1002/yd.20230

often the magnified outcome of students' social media use to share dissatisfaction and seek justice (2016). Social media have become the backbone of accountability for students to hold their institutions of education responsible (New, 2016). While universities are figuring out how to respond, social networking sites allow students to listen to each other, demonstrate their solidarity with each other, and lead with each other through activism.

Throughout history, fighting injustice has been the curriculum of the college student; through activism students "hold a mirror up to our faces and ask us to *see this*" (Rue, personal communication, February 6, 2016). In 1970, Ellsworth and Burns claimed student activism was as American as apple pie and dated its origins to dissatisfied students at Harvard in 1638. In her 2010 dissertation, Rosas traces the history of student activism and defines it as the involvement in demonstrations, where there is a strong commitment to engagement in political and social changes toward social justice. In her 2016 Dalton Institute keynote speech, Wake Forest University Vice President Penny Rue reminded attendees, "It was students who sat in at the Greensboro lunch counters, students who shut down college campuses across the nation after the invasion of Cambodia, students who promoted divestment of companies doing business in Apartheid South Africa" (personal communication, February 6, 2016). Although student activism may be as old as time, how it has transformed through technology is a radical shift in our time.

Digital and technological advances in the 21st century encompass a vast array of changes. Specific to students in the millennial generation and their approach to activism, this chapter focuses on the digital advances of social media and social networking online platforms. In particular, this chapter identifies three characteristics of digitally aided student activism and presents three case studies applicable to leadership educators.

Characteristics of Digitally Aided Movements

Recent digitally aided movements are characterized by three shared traits each of which has helped to define the growth of student activism. These traits are visible within the case studies explored later in this chapter, each of which provide tangible examples of the characteristics that drive social media-aided activist efforts.

First, these movements have largely been nonhierarchical and often described as leaderless (Grinberg, 2014; Schradie, 2014). This structural trait is not to say that movements such as Black Lives Matter and Occupy Wall Street have not had participants that were central to the development and growth of activity, but rather the movements were (and are) a level structure with many leaders. Participants in these efforts have mostly defined their own respective levels of involvement and as a result, it is often difficult to identify one or more individuals who sit at the top of any structure.

NEW DIRECTIONS FOR STUDENT LEADERSHIP • DOI: 10.1002/yd

A second shared characteristic of recent student activism is the use of digital platforms for organizing. Organizing in this context can be thought of as both the act of distributing and arranging logistical tasks and managing the flow of relevant news and information around a movement into and out of the group of activists (Tufekci & Wilson, 2012). In terms of logistical organizing, the online connections between individuals allow for causes and activists to be discovered and paired easily. This ability to organize easily online can be seen in many ways, from Facebook event pages to Twitter accounts that call for specific needs to easily shareable images that contain organizing information.

Finally, these movements have also been characterized by the public use of iterative processes to achieve shared language and develop goals. Through social media, today's activists have embraced open debate. These issues at hand, both large and small, play out across forums that allow for public input. As a result, one can see how issues move from conception through various stages of change and into a firmer or finalized state. It is a cycle that includes presentation, critique, and refining, and it allows for wide-scale participation among a membership. These processes can be seen in tangible ways from the emergent hashtags of movements to the specific calls for action that arise from protests. Through public, iterative processes, participants are empowered to help shape movements alongside their peers.

Case Studies

The cases addressed in this chapter include Occupy Wall Street, which began away from any particular college campus yet included many current students and quickly grew within many college towns (Gismondi, 2014). Also addressed are the 2012 tuition protests in Quebec, which occurred in direct response to issues surrounding the cost of higher education and an attempted quelling of student organizing rights (Kennelly, 2014). Finally, this chapter looks at the recent events at the University of Missouri as part of the larger Black Lives Matter movement. This case study brings in issues of campus climate, student activism, and university responsibility in the face of student unrest (Somashekhar, 2015). All three of these case studies illustrate the power of amplification that mobile and social technologies provide to today's activist students.

Occupy Wall Street.   Occupy Wall Street emerged at the intersection of national political unrest and an evolving media that allowed for new methods of activism. Although the earliest days of the Occupy movement were not set within a particular university environment, the cause can be understood as a student (and educator) driven movement in many ways (Gismondi, 2014). A survey of participants in a May 2011 Occupy rally found 24% current students and 39% more already holding degrees (Milkman, Luce, & Lewis, 2013). Student involvement in Occupy could also be seen through the coverage within college media outlets

(Reimold, 2011), college town social media activity (Caren & Gaby, 2011), and within one of the central grievances of the activists, the call for relief from the tremendous amount of student debt held nationally (Declaration of the Occupation, 2011). Among Occupy participants, one survey found that greater than 50% of respondents under age 30 had over $1,000 in student debt at the time (Milkman et al., 2013).

From the earliest days of Occupy Wall Street, social media platforms helped to define the movement. Along with the early blog posts that helped to begin framing the cause and start the organizing, a single account on Tumblr, *We Are the 99 Percent*, helped to launch Occupy into the mainstream. The Tumblr page, which featured user-submitted images of individuals holding signs that told personal stories of economic strife, was a driving force behind the Occupy narrative that the average person was facing unprecedented difficulty due to the few powerful individuals at the top of the societal hierarchy. Almost immediately after it was started, the Tumblr account gathered followers in large numbers (Caren & Gaby, 2011). Although there were a few early participants who set general terms of the Occupy movement, members were able to bring personal narratives into the cause in a way that the movement adapted and grew iteratively to suit the needs and demands of the activists.

Across the timeline of the Occupy movement, the Tumblr and blog posts served as one portion of a larger social media strategy that included highly active Facebook, Twitter, and YouTube accounts, each of which drove activism in distinct ways. Twitter and Facebook accounts were used to organize offline time-specific events including information regarding event locations and other logistics; needs of Occupy sites (including logistical Twitter accounts for particular cities); and information dissemination, in terms of both internal information and big picture news stories that related to the movement. YouTube allowed for participants to record important moments as they occurred across all Occupy locations and they offered an immersive experience even to activists who were unable to physically attend offline gatherings and protest events. Once the larger Occupy community connected with the primary social media hubs, information flow was instantaneous and direct. This allowed for these tools to serve the needs of the organizers on a minute-to-minute basis. This democratized nature of Occupy is a product of both the movement's core messaging and the central use of social media to build and grow that messaging.

Quebec Tuition Protests.   In early 2012, the government of the Canadian province of Quebec proposed an increase in college student tuition. Under this plan, tuition would increase by $254 each year for 7 years with later increases tied to the rate of inflation. Established student organizations were quick to mobilize students upset with this tuition hike, and by March of 2012 protests began around Quebec.

The protests in the early spring grew and amidst accounts of violence between the protestors and the local law enforcement, the provincial

NEW DIRECTIONS FOR STUDENT LEADERSHIP • DOI: 10.1002/yd

government passed Bill 78, which sought to slow the protestors. The controversial bill imposed a number of restrictions on public demonstrations (Smith, 2012) and imposed fines on protestors who blocked access to schools (Kennelly, 2014). The passage of Bill 78 brought greater attention and public support for the student protestors and nightly protests in May 2012 grew to include more than 150,000 participants.

The Quebec tuition protests amplified and organized on a minute-to-minute basis through social media. The Quebec student activists relied on social media as an organizing tool through a combination of internal information dissemination including the coordination of meeting locations, and external public outreach. By actively engaging on social media platforms, participants developed a movement that was highly interactive, broader, and more effectual. The notion of accessibility with regards to smartphones and social media was essential in providing real-time updates to participants and outside observers alike (Wyatt, 2012).

The movement became known as the Maple Spring and took on a broader message of social justice and equality across topics including the environment, democratic representation, and the prioritization of society over corporate influence (Nadeau-Dubois, 2015). Although education messaging and the central demand to keep tuition fixed remained, the widened dialogue developed as a result of the democratized, participant-driven, iterative process. This process occurred offline and online with many of the student organizations offering French and English language websites and social media posts. The iterative process can also be seen through the use of (often humorous) memes and shared language. The memes, which often used popular imagery from the Internet, carried serious undertones calling for fair treatment from government officials and demanding change. These images of protestors carrying signs of memes, or wearing the movement's symbolic red square badge of unity, were then shared back on the social media pages of activists, thus allowing for messaging to travel across different media and for participants to change, remix, and further develop the messages. This form of digitally aided dialogue was also present within the development of student activist hashtags, including #casserolesencours, which referred to the use of casserole dishes as marching drums in the streets. Journalists within the province reported the student use of digital tools, including social media, allowed activists to act deftly and communicate mostly away from the view of government officials (Wyatt, 2012). Although much of the organizing happened in public, digital spaces, officials were not prepared to react and engage effectively online.

Black Lives Matter (BLM) at the University of Missouri.   In response to the growing national sentiment that young people of color were at constant risk of police brutality and unjust treatment within the legal system, an organized movement became visible in 2013. The particular case that brought the issue to public attention was the acquittal of George Zimmerman in the death of Trayvon Martin, a young Black teenager. After this trial, the hashtags #BlackLivesMatter and #BLM began to circulate as a way for people to share their anguish (Ginwright, 2015). By the fall of 2014, with tensions already on the rise, Michael Brown, an 18-year-old from the St. Louis suburb of Ferguson, was fatally shot by a police officer. This event set off a series of rallies in the city and the state of Missouri; in the fall of 2015, the University of Missouri became the epicenter of BLM.

Multiple issues contributed to demonstrations at the University of Missouri, including racial issues, the treatment of graduate students and university employees, and anger against university leadership inaction. Perhaps the major turning point came on September 12, 2015, when student government president Payton Head wrote a Facebook post outlining his personal experiences regarding the hostile racial climate on campus including racist epithets that had been yelled at him, and called for change. Through the social media platform, Head's post was shared 645 times within the first two days of posting (Serven, 2015).

In the weeks that followed Head's Facebook posting, students organized protests focused on the administration's lack of action in response to the larger campus climate. During this period, several more racially motivated acts occurred, including property damage and the yelling of racial slurs (Pearson, 2015). In November 2015, one student began a hunger strike during which he demanded the resignation of the University of Missouri's president. This action drew more attention and within a week the university's football team announced that they would be boycotting upcoming games. Two days after this announcement, Timothy M. Wolfe, the president of the University of Missouri system, resigned.

Although we have isolated the complicated events at the University of Missouri, the larger context of Black Lives Matter is important to understanding this particular case. Students at the University of Missouri were inspired by and learned from the use of social media as an organizing tool in the Ferguson protests (Eligon & Perez-Pena, 2015). These organizing efforts included sharing news and information relating to local and national issues as well as logistical information about demonstrations and campus action. The movement of Black Lives Matter between local and national issues allowed local organizers to shape the cause and for a national narrative to emerge powered by digital, social platforms. The sharing of live and recorded video, along with citizen journalists capturing actions of both protestors and law enforcement, allowed for participation across state and national borders. As participants watched the movement bloom, they were immersed in the actions of their peers and nationally resonant themes developed. The ability to contribute and follow the actions of peers is also indicative of the flattened structure of the Black Lives Matter movement.

Many of the issues that arose from the Black Lives Matter movement at the University of Missouri evolved over time with a number of concerns relating to education (diversity concerns within faculty and resources in particular) coming to the fore. The dynamics seen during the University of Missouri protests also fit within issues in the national higher education discourse including the tensions between free speech and the incremental nature of change at large institutions, campus journalists, and media coverage of activists. The impact of the events at Missouri highlighted the power of colleges within larger social justice issues, and the actions of the students became a source of learning for current and future college students many of whom now have a model for collective action (Somashekhar, 2015).

Lessons Learned

As we look at recent movements to learn about how technology is influencing student activism, certain themes emerge. First, the successes of the activists highlighted in this chapter galvanized participants through the development of immersive, relatable, and easily shared (via social media) narratives. Each movement began around a core issue but each was flexible enough to allow organic change to happen in terms of messaging and proposed action.

Second, these social media-driven, nonhierarchical student activist movements face the challenge of negotiating change with long-standing, traditional power structures. Problems arise when activists' language and goals evolve and become broad to the point they are unwieldy to administrators seeking actionable change. This is a criticism often levied at the Occupy movement—it helped to mold the public dialogue reaching as far as the highest ranking global politicians, yet did legislation result from the movement? The BLM activists in Missouri brought about significant change in the public dialogue and forced the resignation of their university president, yet significant inequities in higher education (and more broadly, society) still exist. In the Quebec protests, clarity of actionable change resulted in both the resignation of the minister of education and achievement of the initial goal of preventing tuition protests. The power of shifting a national narrative is difficult to overstate, yet the opportunity that widespread attention presents may be the best moment for instituting systemic change. As noted earlier, the iterative nature of online activist dialogue can allow for many participants, but the challenge is in crafting a clear message or set of demands. The outcomes of Occupy, BLM, and Quebec demonstrate the importance of movements to identify and fight for both transformational and clearly defined incremental change.

Third, these movements speak to the complexity of competing desires; as activist causes use social media platforms to grow broadly, activists may splinter or find dissimilar ground within the organization. Again, the ability of social media to serve as a tool for engaging potential participants across a spectrum presents an incredible opportunity but it also means that activists must remain aware that this diversity of opinion can present distinct challenges. In this sense, activists must remain open and aware that these modern movements are built to adapt and change with the groups they represent.

Implications for Practice

Grounded in the experience of these case studies in addition to leadership theory and practice, we offer five specific implications for practice. The five "r's" for practice are *reminder, respect, reality check, relationships*, and *recognition*: a *reminder* to welcome dissent, to *respect* the transformational impact of technology, a *reality check* that you have to be there, the *relationship* potential in your reach, and the *recognition* that online narratives reflect offline pain, joy, and the possibility for transformative social change.

Reminder.   First is a reminder to welcome dissent. As long as student activism has existed, administrators have wrestled with bridging the desired new reality and constraints of the day. And yet, how quickly we become defenders of the constraints. As advocates for both students and universities, we must constantly remind ourselves, "students are not working against the university, but on its behalf. They want to call the university to live up to its mission and its aspirations" (Rue, personal communication, February 6, 2016). Through welcoming dissent, educators can identify adaptive challenges and work collaboratively with students to raise urgency concerning the issue. Forty-five years ago, Ellsworth and Burns (1970) stated, "Activism is not to be feared—on the contrary, it is to be welcomed ... Student activism will not disappear, in fact, it is more likely that the movement will continue to increase in intensity and frequency" (p. 2).

Respect.   Second is a call to respect the transformational impact of technology. Although it is not the *why*, new technologies are the *how* and *what* of student activism and networks. If educators ignore or minimize the transformative power of new technologies, we risk becoming irrelevant in student lives. The digital age is much more than simply an additional form of communication. When ACPA: College Student Educators International (ACPA) and NASPA: Student Affairs Administrators in Higher Education (NASPA) added the technology competency area to Professional Competency Areas for Student Affairs (2015), they did so because they believed student learning and success occur across physical and virtual environments; and beyond hardware and software, technology encompasses innovative, new ways of being for the profession (ACPA & NASPA, 2015). The digital age democratizes and diversifies the creation of knowledge (Hernández, 2015) and exacerbates the need for diversity in staffing and administration (Gismondi, 2015). Which student voices and social issues are brought to the table? Who is being heard? Creating diverse teams is critical to creating relevant and just educational environments—social media only enhances this priority.

Reality Check.   Third is a reality check: *you* have to be there. We must be in the virtual spaces where students are constructing, editing, and reacting to new knowledge. Although this may be a generational issue that will eventually solve itself, we cannot risk waiting for luddites to retire. In the gap between now and then, we risk losing the trust of our most sacred community members. Through participation in the digital world, educators have the opportunity to listen and learn from voices they may not otherwise have had the opportunity to hear. Key positional leaders with authority are often the last to know what is happening on the front lines of student lives. Authority can blind us from the stories we most need to hear; in online worlds, students are speaking truth to power daily in ways they do not have the opportunity to do in person. By being there, we not only listen and understand student needs, we can build trust by responding with care and action-oriented solutions. New technologies provide both students and administrators access to each other and break down the barriers of communication created through the hierarchies of educational systems. Through engaging, nurturing, and sustaining constant dialogue with students in virtual spaces, we can transform our physical spaces.

Relationship.   Fourth is the opportunity to build relationships with students before the protests begin. Our presence in digital spaces allows us to open up the dialogue before it occurs across lines of animosity. Student postings may initially begin as a cathartic process or because they feel it is their only means of being heard, and our ability to be there, to listen, and to respond may lead to discussion and collaboration instead of exacerbating feelings of only-ness and isolation (New, 2016). Social networking sites provide the opportunity not only to let students know they are heard but also that we are doing something about what we have heard. More important, administrators and educators do not have to wait to respond. We can instigate these relationships and build trust by the messages we post in the digital world. If students audited your online presence, what would they assume your values to be? Would they assume you care about the issues they face? How do you advocate and create spaces that let all students know they matter to you? Simply through what you post, you are sending messages that either build or break down trust and either lay the foundation for or create barriers to relationships with students you may never meet offline.

Recognition.   Finally, recognition acknowledges that online narratives are part of real life and reflect offline pain, joy, and the possibility for transformative social change. What we read and witness online are indicators of actual experiences and needs (Hernández, 2015). Although it may be easier to assume overly dramatic interpretations of self, students are actually showing up more authentically than not when online (Hernández, 2015). This recognition calls us to read, respond to, and enhance our lessons learned from student activity online and to trust the messages they are sending us concerning their anger and frustration as well as their joy and celebrations. If students are posting about it, they are thinking about it, and most significantly, they want to talk about it. Instead of student surveys to capture programming ideas, educators can do a quick online check to identify trending topics. Themes captured from social media are ripe for campus programming to dive deeper into the conversation. If they are discussing online, they are seeking the conversation offline and in other formats (Hernández, 2015; Smith, 2013).

Our capacity to remember the power of dissent, respect the transformative nature of technology, check our dismissiveness and get online, use our online presence to create relationships, and recognize the truth and insight in what we learn will allow us to become better partners with student activists. This partnership allows us to effectively serve as a bridge between our current realities and desired futures. If we can do this, then our campus communities will serve as models of evolutionally change because as Angus Johnson describes, we are "big enough to matter but small enough to have an influence on" (Wong, 2015, p. 7).

Concluding Thoughts

The future of research within student activism in a digital age will depend largely on the movements yet to come. Scholars and practitioners would be wise to carefully track social media trends on both local and national levels in order to identify coming activist movements. The proliferation of new digital tools to sort and track data on social media will present new opportunities for these scholars, as activist centers will likely be easier to recognize early in their growth. The archival nature of social media presents another opportunity for digital scholars as all or most of online activity will be possible to record and analyze. In order to encourage growth, recent movements have chosen public-facing media platforms including Twitter, Facebook, YouTube, and so forth. These applications allow for an unprecedented depth of data collection and organization that should aid predictive modeling and qualitative understanding of participant motives.

Beyond shared knowledge and perspectives, the possibility for educational institutions to practice the mission-based outcomes we espouse will be significantly informed by these digitally aided movements. As student activists continue to leverage technology to advance causes, educators and administrators will begin to see not only larger trends in student activist behavior but also individual cases that will inform our educational practice, programs, and policies. Locally and globally student activists are creating opportunities for educational institutions to become equitable, just learning environments; through technology, they are doing so at a pace that is outrunning us. Just imagine if administrators could harness and learn new technologies as fast as our students; think of the transformational change we could create together.

References

ACPA: College Student Educators International & NASPA: Student Affairs Administrators in Higher Education. (2015). *ACPA/NASPA professional competency areas for student affairs practitioners* (2nd ed.). Washington, DC: Authors.

Caren, N., & Gaby, S. (2011, October 24). Occupy online: Facebook and the spread of Occupy Wall Street. Retrieved from http://ssrn.com/abstract=1943168 or http://dx.doi.org/10.2139/ssrn.1943168

Declaration of the Occupation of New York City. (2011). In *#OCCUPYWALLSTREET: New York City General Assembly*. Retrieved from http://www.nycga.net/resources/documents/declaration/

Eligon, J., & Pérez-Peña, R. (2015, November 9). University of Missouri protests spur a day of change. *New York Times*. Retrieved from http://www.nytimes.com/2015/11/10/us/university-of-missouri-system-president-resigns.html?_r=0

Ellsworth, F. L., & Burns, M. A. (1970). *Student activism in American higher education* (Student Personnel Series #10). Washington, DC: ACPA.

Ginwright, S. A. (2015). Radically healing black lives: A love note to justice. In M. P. Evans & K. Knight Abowitz (Eds.), *New Directions for Student Leadership: No. 148. Engaging youth in leadership for social and political change* (pp. 33–44). San Francisco, CA: Jossey-Bass.

Gismondi, A. (2014). #OccupyWallStreet: Social media, education, and the Occupy movement. In V. Benson & S. Morgan (Eds.), *Cutting-edge technologies and social media use in higher education* (pp. 156–172). London, England: IGI Global.

Gismondi, A. (2015). *#CivicEngagement: An exploratory study of social media use and civic engagement among undergraduates* (Unpublished doctoral dissertation). Chestnut Hill, MA: Boston College.

Grinberg, E. (2014, November 19). How #Ferguson became a social media rallying call. CNN. Retrieved from http://www.cnn.com/2014/11/19/us/ferguson-social-media-injustice/

Hernández, E. (2015). #hermandad: Twitter as a counter-space for Latina doctoral students. *Journal of College and Character*, 16(2), 124–130. doi:10.1080/2194587X.2015.1024795

Kennelly, J. (2014). The Quebec student protests: Challenging neoliberalism one pot at a time. *Critical Arts*, 28, 135–139. doi:10.1080/02560046.2014.883699

Milkman, R., Luce, S., & Lewis, P. (2013). *Changing the subject: A bottom-up account of Occupy Wall Street in New York City*. New York, NY: CUNY.

Nadeau-Dubois, G. (2015). *In defiance*. Toronto, ON: Lazer Lederhendler.

New, J. (2016, May 13). Students turn to Twitter, Facebook with sexual assault complaints. *Inside Higher Ed*. Retrieved from https://www.insidehighered.com/news/2016/05/13/students-turn-twitter-facebook-sexual-assault-complaints/

Pearson, M. (2015, November 10). A timeline of the University of Missouri protests. CNN. Retrieved from http://www.cnn.com/2015/11/09/us/missouri-protest-timeline/

Reimold, D. (2011, October 13). Occupy Wall Street: Student press perspectives on the protests. *College Media Matters*. Retrieved from http://collegemediamatters.com/2011/10/13/occupy-wall-street-student-press-perspectives-on-the-protests/

Rosas, M. (2010). *College student activism: An exploration of learning outcomes*. (Doctoral dissertation). Iowa City: University of Iowa. Retrieved from http://ir.uiowa.edu/etd/589

Schradie, J. (2014, November 3). Bringing the organization back in: Social media and social movements. *Berkeley Journal of Sociology*. Retrieved from: http://berkeleyjournal.org/2014/11/bringing-the-organization-back-in-social-media-and-social-movements/

Serven, R. (2015, September 14). MSA president speaks out about racist incident. *Columbia Missourian*. Retrieved from http://www.columbiamissourian.com/news/higher_education/msa-president-speaks-out-about-racist-incident/article_ac4ebc2c-5b3e-11e5-b4bd-af55f13bae45.html

Smith, A. (2013, April 25). Civic engagement in the digital age. *Pew Research Center*. Retrieved from http://www.pewinternet.org/2013/04/25/civic-engagement-in-the-digital-age/

Smith, C. (2012, May 21). Montreal protesters defy demo law and clash with police. *CBC News*. Retrieved from http://www.cbc.ca/news/canada/montreal/montreal-protesters-defy-demo-law-and-clash-with-police-1.1279274

Somashekhar, S. (2015, November 17). How Black Lives Matter, born on the streets, is rising to power on campus. *Washington Post*. Retrieved from https://www.washingtonpost.com/national/how-black-lives-matter-born-on-the-streets-is-rising-to-power-on-campus/2015/11/17/3c113e96-8959-11e5-be8b-1ae2e4f50f76_story.html

Tufekci, Z., & Wilson, C. (2012). Social media and the decision to participate in political protest: Observations from Tahrir Square. *Journal of Communication, 62*, 363–379. doi:10.1111/j.1460-2466.2012.01629.x

Wong, A. (2015, May 21). The renaissance of student activism. *Atlantic*. Retrieved from http://www.theatlantic.com/education/archive/2015/05/the-renaissance-of-student-activism/393749/

Wyatt, N. (2012, June 18). Social media breaks new ground in Quebec protests. *Metro News Canada*. Retrieved from http://www.metronews.ca/news/canada/2012/06/18/social-media-breaks-new-ground-in-protests.html

ADAM GISMONDI serves as program administrator at the Tufts University Institute for Democracy and Higher Education and as a visiting scholar at Boston College. He holds a PhD in higher education from Boston College and is an advisory board member for SXSWedu.

LAURA OSTEEN serves as the director of the Center for Leadership and Social Change at Florida State University. An advocate of student activism and amateur of digital technology, Laura seeks to realize and amplify their synergy for positive sustainable change.

New Directions for Student Leadership • DOI: 10.1002/yd

6

This chapter reviews the complex relationship between technology and leadership, focusing on how technology affects the development and demonstration of skills in communication, teamwork, and collaboration. The chapter also proposes a framework for identifying and assessing key leadership competencies in the digital space.

The Virtual Table: A Framework for Online Teamwork, Collaboration, and Communication

Lisa Endersby, Kirstin Phelps, Dan Jenkins

The impact of technology on leaders and leadership development in higher education is no longer a rare, one-off event. A leader cannot solely be identified by the loudest voice at the table or the most towering presence in the room as anyone with an Internet connection and a computer (or smartphone or tablet) can type or text their way to a leadership role or emerge as a leader (Yoo & Alavi, 2004). A diversity of technology platforms and tools have created a new space for collaboration and teamwork we have termed the "virtual table"—a place in which both students and educators must be grounded in knowledge, yet innovative in their approach to learning, often simultaneously and without a foundational set of guidelines. Leaders must also contend with a virtual table that exists in multiple "rooms" and can seat multiple people for a variety of purposes.

This chapter recommends relevant implications for practice by focusing on leading a team using digital technology around a virtual table. To narrow the scope of this chapter, leadership is conceived of as the behaviors of any individual (both with or without formal authority) who seeks to influence the direction of the group. Further, this chapter focuses on exploring the gaps in practice-oriented literature related to (a) *power and platform* (how leaders can gain, maintain, and lose traditionally held indicators of power online); (b) *presence* (how leaders build and maintain an active, highly visible presence online and whether this constant visibility is necessary for effective leadership); and (c) *participation* (how leaders

New Directions for Student Leadership, no. 153, Spring 2017 © 2017 Wiley Periodicals, Inc., A Wiley Company
Published online in Wiley Online Library (wileyonlinelibrary.com) • DOI: 10.1002/yd.20231

actively engage with a team that may be able to remain productive without their constant, vigilant attention).

Considerations of Virtual Leadership

In practice, leadership can be defined as "a solution to the problem of collective effort—the problem of bringing people together and combining their efforts to promote success and survival" (Kaiser, Hogan, & Craig, 2008, p. 96). The workplace and the classroom provide valuable spaces for the emergence and nurturing of attitudes and competencies in support of this collective effort—teachers, students, workers, and bosses have ample access to a diverse set of resources while working toward a common goal. Leaders are identified based on frequent, overt displays of leadership behaviors. Additionally, their status (positional or otherwise) is continuously reinforced in the social hierarchy of the office or classroom. In the face-to-face (F2F), physical environment, leaders have ready access to the formal structures and informal, assumed social dynamics that allow them to capture and maintain their high status or influence within the group.

However, many of these structures, networks, and social cues can be greatly enhanced or be noticeably absent within a virtual setting. Emerging as a leader online, often in the context of online learning communities, can mean emerging as an opinion leader capable of using one's "superior status, education, and social prestige ... to influence followers" (Li, Ma, Zhang, & Huang, 2013, p. 43). Social network researchers describe this phenomenon as the "majority illusion" (Lerman, Yan, & Wu, 2016, p. 1). A number of contagious behaviors, such as the spread of fads, memes, social norms, or public opinions, are often precipitated by a small group of central individuals (i.e., opinion leaders) whose behaviors are more easily spread to the larger population due to their central location and large audience. However, centrality is just one indicator of status within social networks. An individual who is seen as having a high level of expertise in a particular area, combined with personality traits often ascribed to a leader (e.g., extroversion and assertiveness) (Katz, 1957), can also attain the status of opinion leader in a virtual space. Satisfaction with and trust in the ascribed opinion leader, however, can vary based on different settings, with research supporting the continued importance of matching a leadership style (e.g., transactional or transformational) to task type (e.g., short-term projects) across F2F, hybrid, and online work environments (Hoyt & Blascovich, 2003). The judgment of a leader as a content expert is also challenging in the virtual environment, with the majority of research surrounding opinion leaders as experts focusing on the possession of technical knowledge that can be easily confirmed as right or wrong (e.g., Wikipedia, Google). The interplay of perceived expertise and the socioemotional status markers of leadership represent emerging opportunities for leadership development in an online environment.

Interactions in the online space can often be devoid of the valuable social cues that permeate more emotionally and personality-driven leadership styles. In many cases, group members may use pseudonyms to feel a sense of safety in their interactions and conversations, hoping to mitigate the risk of damaging their "real life" reputation (Ross, 2007) while simultaneously making it challenging for a leader to develop strong social ties and, consequently, a more authoritative virtual presence.

A virtual leader must also work to demonstrate their authority without the benefit of recognition or response from others from more traditional signals of power. Effective virtual leadership, then, requires the careful coordination and intersection of the social underpinnings and knowledge-sharing networks because members of online communities will often seek out and establish social connections in order to share knowledge in an environment based on trust and care (Von Krogh, 2002). Virtual leadership is further complicated by notions of distributed leadership wherein an online community could identify multiple members as leaders in a space devoid of traditional behavioral indicators of hierarchy and more commonly understood organizational structures (Purvanova & Bono, 2009).

Standards and Competencies for Virtual Leadership

As student learning and success transcend physical and virtual domains, leadership development must be considered and supported equally across both physical and digital environments. In all aspects and on all platforms, the virtual enactment of leadership has additional complexity such that competencies related to group initiation, motivation, and maintaining the structure of a (physical or virtual) team require personal reflection and awareness of one's collaborative interactions in the digital space (Mukherjee, Lahiri, Mukherjee, & Billing, 2012). Accordingly, a discussion of virtual team leadership must be grounded in an understanding of leadership as it applies to this unique context. The Council for the Advancement of Standards in Higher Education (CAS, 2015) developed a series of standards for multiple functional areas in higher education, including student leadership programs, in an attempt to narrow the scope of leadership development for practical use by educators and administrators and reflect good practices in student leadership programming. As leadership research and practice continues to evolve, technology has played a role in reforming and envisioning how leadership programs are developed, facilitated, and assessed.

A Continuum for Team Virtuality

Although it may be easier to describe virtual teams in comparison to in-person teams, the reality is that most teams, regardless of place or setting, engage with technology in some capacity. Rather than considering only the binary distinction of virtual *or* F2F groups, team virtuality should instead be considered along a fluid continuum. On the online extreme, team members are remote and meet exclusively through text and/or video conferencing software. On the F2F extreme, team members engage in the physical space such as a classroom, but may still use collaborative tools, such as Trello or Google docs, to organize their work. In between are hybrid teams; for example, blended learning classrooms or collaborative student groups who may meet a few times F2F and also conduct much of their daily business through technology.

In each of these cases, *where* the team is situated along the continuum has important considerations for leadership, for virtual leaders, and for the different ways leadership dimensions—such as social power and prestige, topic expertise, and adaptive facilitation—may be expressed. The need for virtual leadership competency could therefore be enacted differently based upon where the team is situated within the range of virtuality (Table 6.1).

In considering these dimensions of virtuality, we can see that a number of guidelines put forth by the CAS (2015) standards are just as important to develop in real as in virtual space. And, although we stand to learn from how virtual competencies such as process orientation, cultural and geographical considerations, accessibility, engagement, and communication are assessed in other contexts, no measurable criteria exist to assess virtual student leadership specifically. The following section of this chapter integrates the key considerations emerging from dialogue around student leadership and technology competencies into a framework through which educators can begin to assess these skills across the multivariate contexts in which leadership and virtual collaboration occurs.

Virtual Leadership Considerations

Given the continuum of team environments and technology described previously, what does a "successful" or a "functional/productive" virtual team look like? Imagine a group of students, collaborating to solve a problem or complete a specific task. The task itself—whether academic or social in nature—is less important than how individuals engage in the collaborative process: what technologies they choose to use, what skills they employ, and the environment in which they interact. First, the group must, by direction of a leader or collaboratively, decide on the appropriate information and communication technologies (ICTs) to meet and work through the problem or task. To be effective, this decision-making process must consider a number of dimensions: (a) access and power dimensions of technology, (b) social and technical processes, (c) engagement and inclusivity of group members, (d) adaptability, and (e) how the entire process will be facilitated. For example, what does it mean to have a conversation about the goals of the group and align them to technological resources? Although a Google doc may be ideal for certain tasks, what about when trying to delegate subtasks, reach consensus, or brainstorm? Moreover, what are the implications

NEW DIRECTIONS FOR STUDENT LEADERSHIP • DOI: 10.1002/yd

Table 6.1   A Continuum of Team Virtuality

	Online	Hybrid	Face to Face
	⬅——————————————➡		
Social Power and Prestige	Power gained through status as opinion leader	Physical signals of power or assigned position of authority	Physical (traditional) signals of power
	Online environment influences expressions of power	Prestige partly based on frequency of communication	Assigned position of authority
Topic Expertise	Veracity of content compared to other widely available socially constructed knowledge	Online tools provide valuable medium to quickly review large volumes of information	Veracity of content measured against established knowledge of team and members
		Face-to-face interactions can offer additional opportunities to evaluate content	
Adaptive Facilitation	Technology can help (e.g., efficiency) and hinder (e.g., capacity) effective facilitation	Demands frequent shifts in facilitation style(s) to account for movement between online and face-to-face environments	Relies heavily on visible body language and other cues to adapt facilitation style
	Facilitator must be skilled in both use of technology and facilitation across virtual platforms	Demonstration and identification of important social cues for adaptive facilitation vary between settings	Challenges can be mitigated with on the spot strategies

of each technological decision for privacy, security, engagement, and capturing members' contributions? Likewise, what outcomes are affected if members are unfamiliar with, or do not fully understand, dimensions of a technology they are supposed to employ?

The following section introduces a Virtual Leadership Competency Framework, designed with great intentionality to develop key dimensions of leadership for students who will be called to lead in virtual environments. Although the CAS (2015) standards have helped provide teaching, learning, and assessment strategies for leadership development programming, a gap exists in translating these guidelines into virtual settings. For example, in an exploratory study among leadership courses, Jenkins (2016) found online courses weighted group assessment strategies 12th (out of 17), compared to in-person courses that weighted similar strategies of group work and group presentations the heaviest. All other factors remaining the same (e.g., course type or subject matter), why are instructors excluding group work in their online classes? Are aspiring leaders who take online classes less expected to work in virtual teams? Of course not. It is our responsibility as leadership educators to identify emerging techniques and innovative approaches to teaching in virtual environments (Andenoro et al., 2013). The Virtual Leadership Competency Framework (Table 6.2), represents an initial operationalization around how to assess and evaluate students' skill development around virtual leadership and collaboration.

Virtual Leadership Competency Framework

The framework guides leadership educators to integrate emerging technology standards with proposed virtual leadership competencies by providing suggestions for assessment and pedagogical application. Motivation for the framework was not so much *if* students will be engaging with others through technology, but rather *how* can we best prepare them to do so while considering power and platform, presence, and participation.

The integration of technology centers upon four key considerations of virtual leadership competency represented in the framework: (a) adaptive facilitation, (b) understanding technological amplifications of power, (c) recognition of integrated social-technical processes, and (d) nuanced understanding of technology.

Key Consideration #1: Adaptive Facilitation.   The adaptive facilitation required for virtual leadership competency is reflected in the ability of team leaders to support and facilitate team processes. This involves developing in students an understanding of and orientation toward the four key considerations when enacting leadership within virtual settings. It is not enough to encourage the use of "appropriate" technology; which technology is "appropriate" is determined by team factors as well as individual competency and familiarity with the technology at hand.

Collaborative technologies do not support collaboration if team members do not see them as collaborative (Orlikowski, 1992). Furthermore, team technology choice and, ultimately, team performance are affected by a number of team characteristics, including digital literacy proficiency, comfort level, and mental models around technologies. In order to increase the effectiveness of technology, team characteristics must align with their collaborative use. The team communication tool, Slack, will not be effective if not all team members are familiar or comfortable using it. However, it is often too easy to make assumptions about technology proficiency, efficacy, or access in today's digital age.

Adaptive facilitation that considers group dimensions around technology is an important leadership role and skill set in virtual team settings. For

Table 6.2   Virtual Leadership Competency Framework

Leadership Competency	Assessment and Evaluation	Pedagogical Application
Adaptive facilitation	Provides coaching and support for group to adopt/implement new technologies Shows awareness of different technological dimensions Incorporates appropriate tech platforms according to team needs	Problem-based learning to pair ICTs with social variables and team goals 360-degree feedback Case studies that highlight implications of ICTs on processes and group dynamics Simulation or role play to reproduce virtual team conflicts and/or communications Team-building activities, simulation, and role-play games
Understanding of technological amplifications of power	Reflects critical understanding of how technological tools may inhibit or promote normative assumptions Combats technological solutions to societal challenges Recognizes technological affordances may privilege and obscure different types of group participation	Include examination of technological components within case studies of leadership Provide historical, illustrative examples of how technology has empowered or disempowered social action Uncover and debrief dominant assumptions about technology connected to collective action and engagement Comparing and contrasting social media platforms with respect to power, influence, social justice, and access Consider examples of power and influence in virtual settings

(Continued)

Table 6.2   Continued

Leadership Competency	Assessment and Evaluation	Pedagogical Application
Recognition of integrated social-technical processes	Respects individual and team concerns around privacy and security on technology-enabled platforms Supports team learning around technology use Initiates team practice and reflection around technology Respects and recognizes individual differences in technological skill Considers social context and group norms around technology use Evaluates how well technology used matched group dimensions	Challenge technical solutions to team challenges Identify and bring attention to technocentric thinking Role model team learning processes within classroom Small group breakouts and discussion Host technology shares for peer teaching by team members
Nuanced understanding of technology	Shows an understanding of the benefits and challenges of ICTs Chooses platforms and applications based upon understanding of group dimensions Sets expectations within group around technology use, team planning, and individual member characteristics	Include technology choice and competency options within self and peer evaluations Discuss how enacted leadership roles may appear in virtual settings Address frequency, responsibility, and expectations around communication

example, supporting team learning through motivation, practice, and reflection has been found to overcome obstacles around new technology adoption (Edmondson, Bohmer, & Pisano, 2001). As a result, the development of adaptive facilitation competencies can be supported by helping students develop awareness for social support roles around technology adoption and how to use them within their group, as well as building awareness of differences among technologies that may affect group work. From an education standpoint, these competencies can be developed through inclusion of adaptive facilitation dimensions through problem-based learning, team building applications, and reflection, among others, which encourages development of awareness toward technology, and technological implications for group work among students.

Key Consideration #2: Understanding Technological Amplifications of Power. As with F2F leadership development, attention to power dynamics are just as important, if not more so, for virtual settings, given assumptions about technology and the lack of overt social cues. A major assumption to challenge is related to the dominant narrative of technocentrism within modern society. Technocentrism (Papert, 1990) is a belief in the power of technology reflected in discourse that promotes scientific and technical solutions as *the* solution to societal problems. How often do we see commercials presenting the newest app, gadget, or device as changing lives? How many times have we heard, "Isn't there an app for that?" as a solution to a personal challenge? The danger in such thinking is that when technology dominates, it is easier to privilege technological competency and knowledge over other types of wisdom, contribution, or social processes. This mindset often glorifies the cult of technology and positions technology as the salvation to those less fortunate, a position that minimizes, undervalues, and potentially oppresses the intended recipient group.

Power dynamics are also at play in the different compositions of social relationships enabled through technology. Flexible work assignments, contractual labor, and part-time work enabled by information technology (IT) may hold benefits for workers, as has been found in research in virtual work, but can also shift the power relationships between capital and labor (Castells, 2011). Virtual team members may not only become less visible to their teammates but they also become less visible to those in managerial roles and, subsequently, may lose bargaining power as well as experience feelings of physical, mental, and social isolation. Classic work exploring IT in the workplace illustrates how choices around technology could either serve to centralize managerial power or enhance employee participation and intellective skill development (Zuboff, 1988). If the goal of leadership is to support collective effort, it is therefore important to understand how technology is being used, for what purposes, and how social relationships may be affected.

Another consideration for power manifestations is related to digital traces left by virtual interaction. As educators, do we use knowledge of student's time logged into Blackboard as a proxy for participation? Is being able to see team members' contributions through Google docs unequivocally a good thing? Technological tools advertised to aid teamwork, may, in fact, create behaviors where team members use technology to monitor each other's work. Such hybrid systems of surveillance are enabled by the creation of digital trace data, which may conflate quantity with quality and privilege certain types of participation over other, less trackable, contributions. Without examining assumptions around technology, we may too easily be convinced of its positive neutrality and benefits to group work and lose a more holistic view of teamwork processes that leadership education strives to make known to students. Technology is not a neutral tool; rather, it serves as an amplifier for forces within the system depending upon its use

(Toyoma, 2015). Therefore, drawing attention to the different ways power can manifest through technology, educators can help develop critical thinking to fight the dominant narrative of technocentrism and help students question simplistic technical solutions to more complex processes.

Key Consideration #3: Recognition of Integrated Social-Technical Processes.   The third consideration reminds us that technical and social processes are intimately connected (MacKenzie & Wajcman, 1999). Consider the smartphone. If you asked a classroom of students to describe their phone, why they have it, how they used it, what apps they had installed, or query other uses you would likely get diverse answers. These answers reflect the ways technology is integrated into our daily lives, and how its use shapes, and is shaped by, the social relationships and social structures in which students engage.

There is no uniform, one-size-fits-all adoption of technology across contexts. Instead, technology use is reflective of the unique needs, environments, and skills of individuals within the social system in which it is embedded. Indeed, even the adoption of technology is a social process (Rogers, 2010) dependent upon social structures, opinion leaders, and social norms. In supporting virtual group work, consideration of social processes must be considered to leverage technological potential. For example, social forces of homophily, that is, the tendency of people to associate with similar others, can limit the broadcasting potential of social media technologies (McPherson, Smith-Lovin, & Cook, 2001). Virtual communication is bounded by the communities and social groups to which you belong, and, just like in real life, people tend to hang out online with other people who are like them. As a result, online communities often serve as echo chambers for homogenous and polarized groups, which supports the dissemination of certain information while simultaneously constraining the spread of others.

Application of technology does not free us from consideration of social processes. Virtual teams are often seen at a disadvantage compared to face-to-face teams, given the low media richness of digital communication compared to in-person communication. However, findings have shown that as virtual teams gain experience working with one another, they can catch up to the benefits of F2F teams (Alge, Wiethoff, & Klein, 2003). Therefore, understanding how social dynamics engage in virtual spaces, and considering them along with technology choices, is an important question for digital leadership. Competencies that support the appropriate use of technology need to simultaneously consider the underlying social dynamics in which the technology is embedded. Development of this competency involves intentional inclusion of technological skills, familiarity, and understanding within the group, rather than blanket assumptions about technology or technical solutions.

Key Consideration #4: Nuanced Understanding of Technology.   The final question brings us to the consideration of group dimensions that factor into the use of appropriate technology. Knowledge of the myriad applications, programs, software, and platforms is not enough; it is also important to understand the benefits and drawbacks of each choice. Ultimately, this knowledge will be used to identify and employ appropriate technology strategically in support of group work.

Different technological applications and platforms have different strengths and weaknesses based upon their design and inherent affordances. Social media, for example, offer ease and convenience of disseminating information quickly to large groups of individuals, while also being limited by homophily, lack of personalization and direct action, and potential for information overload. The choice of what application to use may vary based upon a number of group dimensions that help align appropriate technology with immediate group needs. The model of task–technology fit suggests that a fit between task, technology, and individual characteristics determines performance (Goodhue & Thompson, 1995). Extrapolated to the group level, it is therefore important to understand not only the task the group is trying to accomplish but also individual characteristics of team members. Is the task information related? Does the group need to reduce uncertainty by gathering information around a particular issue? Or is information available and a decision needs to be made on the best course of action? Does the team need to exchange information (conveyance) or attempt to uncover the meaning of information (convergence)?

Depending on the needs of the group around specific tasks, different media choices and organizational work strategies would be more or less appropriate. Low media synchronicity technologies, such as email or texting, are more appropriate for conveyance, whereas high synchronicity technologies are better suited for convergence, though this may decrease over time as groups become more familiar (Dennis & Valacich, 1999). Virtual leadership competency should therefore include appropriate choice of technology, acknowledging its inherent benefits and drawbacks, with awareness of the social and structural factors that still may impede its effective use.

Conclusion

The act of leading virtual teams, and the greater art of leadership, look different online. Without the more traditional markers of leadership, it has become increasingly challenging for students and administrators to find and maintain a seat around the virtual table. For students in organizations, virtual teamwork does not offer traditional indicators of status, leaving potential and positional leaders to compete with a myriad of other people and platforms for attention and authority. Instead, in the digital space, distributed power is now the truest measure of a leader. Creating and maintaining a strong virtual presence in the shadow of constant and competing demands for attention is now less a measure of a leader's visibility and more their ability to critically examine and present information in a way that indicates critical thought and meaningful reflection. Leaders and all members of a virtual team can take advantage of emerging technology that makes engaging across previously impermeable boundaries easier and faster. The opportunities for the effective distribution of power inherent in a diverse team are also important tools for navigating the challenges that arise in bringing together people and perspectives that, previously, were unable or uninterested in interacting.

Higher education administrators are guided in their own development by standards and assertions of competencies they need to best lead, educate, and facilitate programs. Most notably, the revision of the ACPA: College Student Educators International/NASPA: Student Affairs Administrators in Higher Education Professional Competency Areas for Student Affairs (2015) included a stand-alone technology competency, emphasizing the importance of technology in influencing competency development while also supporting the continued practice of multiple essential skills. This competency highlights the complex intersections of leadership and technology as students (and administrators) must simultaneously develop skills in both areas while remaining sensitive to the cyclical impact each domain has on the other.

The complexities of virtual leadership are a newer phenomenon; administrators must now contend with competing demands for student attention while also learning to navigate these same spaces as potential platforms for learning and development. The ACPA/NASPA technology competency highlights this dynamic well, giving equal space to skills related to troubleshooting software or hardware challenges as for critically assessing information shared online (ACPA/NASPA, 2015). For both professionals and students, the use of technological tools means engaging with others in a space lacking overt social cues and context, which can support various functions and serve multiple purposes (often simultaneously). Although the ACPA/NASPA technology competency looks specifically at educational technology competencies, it does not address leadership development with the same specificity. However, the synthesis between competencies in student leadership development and collaborative technology is arguably the next frontier.

New research in the field will lend itself to opportunities for situating learning outcomes related to leadership (e.g., interpersonal communication, collaboration, and conflict management) in this virtual world. Administrators must now consider how the tools that make their data management more efficient can also greatly affect their pedagogy in what they teach, how they teach it, and how their students interact with them, their peers, and the information they share. What tools will we use to build the seats for our team? Who will be able to, or want to, sit at the table we construct? Future research could include how power dynamics influence the building of and seating at the virtual table, particularly from a social justice lens in how these tools and spaces are accessed. Leadership identity must now also broaden to include one's digital identity, and future scholars will explore how these pieces of ourselves and our student leaders intersect. Textbooks and other resources will need to be updated to reflect this changing reality, and including digital identity and mentorship as part of leadership development programming will become a necessary part of how we educate leaders to exist, and thrive, in this new setting. The pursuit of power and presence is no longer a solitary, upward climb; virtual teamwork has, and will continue to, demand leaders whose reach is lateral as well as lofty, and who can welcome the influx of information, ideas, and individuals who will crowd their virtual table.

References

ACPA: College Student Educators International & NASPA: Student Affairs Professionals in Higher Education. (2015). *Professional competency areas for student affairs educators*. Washington, DC: Authors. Retrieved from http://www.naspa.org/images/uploads/main/ACPA_NASPA_Professional_Competencies_FINAL.pdf

Alge, B. J., Wiethoff, C., & Klein, H. J. (2003). When does the medium matter? Knowledge-building experiences and opportunities in decision-making teams. *Organizational Behavior and Human Decision Processes, 91*, 26–37.

Andenoro, A. C., Allen, S. J., Haber-Curran, P., Jenkins, D. M., Sowcik, M., Dugan, J. P., & Osteen, L. (2013). National Leadership Education research agenda 2013–2018: Providing strategic direction for the field of leadership education. Retrieved from http://leadershipeducators.org/ResearchAgenda

Castells, M. (2011). *The rise of the network society: The information age: Economy, society, and culture* (Vol. 1). Oxford, UK: John Wiley & Sons.

Council for the Advancement of Standards in Higher Education. (2015). *CAS professional standards for higher education* (9th ed.). Washington, DC: Author.

Dennis, A. R., & Valacich, J. S. (1999, January). Rethinking media richness: Towards a theory of media synchronicity. In *proceedings from HICSS-32: The 32nd Annual Hawaii International Conference on System Sciences*. Los Alamitos, CA: IEEE Computer Society Press.

Edmondson, A. C., Bohmer, R. M., & Pisano, G. P. (2001). Disrupted routines: Team learning and new technology implementation in hospitals. *Administrative Science Quarterly, 46*, 685–716.

Goodhue, D. L., & Thompson, R. L. (1995). Task-technology fit and individual performance. *MIS Quarterly, 19*, 213–236.

Hoyt, C. L., & Blascovich, J. (2003). Transformational and transactional leadership in virtual and physical environments. *Small Group Research, 34*, 678–715.

Jenkins, D. M. (2016). Teaching leadership online: An exploratory study of instructional and assessment strategy use. *Journal of Leadership Education, 15*(2), 129–149. Retrieved from http://journalofleadershiped.org/index.php/volume-15-issue-2/431-teaching-leadership-online-an-exploratory-study-of-instructional-and-assessment-strategy-use

Kaiser, R. B., Hogan, R., & Craig, S. B. (2008). Leadership and the fate of organizations. *American Psychologist, 63*, 96–110.

Katz, E. (1957). The two-step flow of communication: An up-to-date report on an hypothesis. *Public Opinion Quarterly, 21*, 61–78.

Lerman, K., Yan, X., & Wu, X. (2016). The "majority illusion" in social networks. *PLoS ONE, 11*, 1–13. doi:10.1371/journal.pone.0147617

Li, Y., Ma, S., Zhang, Y., & Huang, R. (2013). An improved mix framework for opinion leader identification in online learning communities. *Knowledge-Based Systems, 43,* 43–51.

MacKenzie, D. A., & Wajcman, J. (1999). The social shaping of technology. In D. A. MacKenzie & J. Wajcman (Eds.), *The social shaping of technology* (2nd ed., pp. 3–27). Buckingham, UK: Open University Press.

McPherson, M., Smith-Lovin, L., & Cook, J. M. (2001). Birds of a feather: Homophily in social networks. *Annual Review of Sociology, 27,* 415–444.

Mukherjee, D., Lahiri, S., Mukherjee, D., & Billing, T. K. (2012). Leading virtual teams: How do social, cognitive, and behavioral capabilities matter? *Management Decision, 50,* 273–290.

Orlikowski, W. (1992). The duality of technology: Rethinking the concept of technology in organizations. *Organization Science, 3,* 398–427.

Papert, S. (1990). *A critique of technocentrism in thinking about the school of the future.* Epistemology and Learning Group, MIT Media Laboratory. Retrieved from http://www.papert.org/articles/ACritiqueofTechnocentrism.html

Purvanova, R. K., & Bono, J. E. (2009). Transformational leadership in context: Face-to-face and virtual teams. *Leadership Quarterly, 20,* 343–357.

Rogers, E. M. (2010). *Diffusion of innovations* (4th ed.). New York, NY: The Free Press.

Ross, D. (2007). Backstage with the knowledge boys and girls: Goffman and distributed agency in an organic online community. *Organization Studies, 28,* 307–325.

Toyoma, K. (2015). *Geek heresy: Rescuing social change from the cult of technology.* New York, NY: Public Affairs.

Von Krogh, G. (2002). The communal resource and information systems. *Journal of Strategic Information Systems, 11,* 85–107.

Yoo, Y., & Alavi, M. (2004). Emergent leadership in virtual teams: What do emergent leaders do? *Information and Organization, 14,* 27–58.

Zuboff, S. (1988). *In the age of the smart machine: The future of work and power.* New York, NY: Basic Books.

LISA ENDERSBY *is a doctoral student exploring professional development in online communities of practice at the University of Windsor. She is past national chair of the NASPA Technology Knowledge Community. Among her numerous publications and presentations is a recent chapter in* Leadership 2050: Critical Challenges, Key Contexts, and Emerging Trends, *by the International Leadership Association (ILA). Lisa is coeditor of "Pause for Pedagogy," a monthly article series in the ILA newsletter exploring innovative pedagogical practices and strategies in leadership education.*

KIRSTIN PHELPS *is a PhD candidate at the iSchool at the University of Illinois at Urbana-Champaign whose research interests include the intersection of information, technology, and leadership, with particular emphasis on social network methods. Previously, she served as an assistant director at the Illinois Leadership Center at the University of Illinois.*

DAN JENKINS *is director and assistant professor of leadership and organizational studies at the University of Southern Maine. His research interests include leadership education, pedagogy, curriculum design and assessment, distance learning, and critical thinking.*

7

This chapter addresses the rapid growth of American industry and a proposed framework—the mindset for career curiosity—that can be used to prepare students for quickly evolving 21st-century digital work environments.

A Mindset for Career Curiosity: Emerging Leaders Working in the Digital Space

Mallory Bower, Peter Konwerski

As technology continues to disrupt industries at a rapid pace, we must address the challenge of preparing students to be leaders who will thrive in increasingly digital workspaces. This chapter explores characteristics of the 21st-century workplace, skills employers seek in college graduates, and a proposed mindset for career curiosity to help students and practitioners to embrace technologies that are evolving the way we work, lead, and live.

Characteristics of the 21st-Century Workplace

The 21st-century workplace is unique for many reasons. The adoption and rapid evolution of technology has changed the way industries become productive and it shapes every sector of society. It has also shined the spotlight on generational differences in the context of work preferences. Just 2 decades ago, the Internet was becoming mainstream and available homes and workplaces. Since then, technology has been changing at such a rapid pace that it has disrupted how we create and share work. Instead of typing this chapter on a Remington typewriter and submitting hard copies for editing, in today's hyperconnected world, it is being written and edited in real time, across two countries and three time zones, and saved in the cloud, something to which current working generations have grown accustomed.

According to the Pew Research Center (Fry, 2015), millennials became the largest share of the American workforce in 2015. Recent U.S. Census data indicate that more than one in three U.S. workers today is a member of the 53.5 million millennial workforce, which just surpassed that of the baby boomers, which has declined as their generation retires.

New Directions for Student Leadership, no. 153, Spring 2017 © 2017 Wiley Periodicals, Inc., A Wiley Company
Published online in Wiley Online Library (wileyonlinelibrary.com) • DOI: 10.1002/yd.20232

Younger employees are bringing technology skills to the workforce that are not always mirrored by their more seasoned peers who can remember a workplace without email or desktop computers (Carnevale & Rose, 2015). Many college students who are transitioning into the world of work may prefer to send text messages than send emails whereas some workforce veterans have just become used to the idea of wired communication. As a result, more employers, organizations, and institutions are spending resources trying to understand younger cohorts of workers and these workers needs, work preferences, and technology competencies.

For instance, according to a Pew Research Center study, 24% of today's teens (ages 13–18) go online "almost constantly" (Lenhart, 2015, p. 2). Mobile technology, including smartphones and tablets, is facilitating shifts in the way students share information and communicate. A connected life is becoming the norm for both teens and adults and it will continue to flatten generational gaps. In fact, 68% of adults now own smartphones and 45% own tablets (Anderson, 2015), which allows employees to work from any place with a wireless Internet connection.

Despite increases in technology use, resistance to change still exists and it can keep technology from positively influencing workflow in productive and measurable ways. Employers and campus administrators need to reimagine environments using a growth mindset (Dweck, 2006; Thomas, 2014), moving leadership practices away from top-down hierarchical bureaucracies and shifting to a more agile, learning-centered, multidirectional team of teachers and learners.

Skills Employers Seek in College Graduates

In academic environments, the liberal arts continue to receive criticism because they do not always lead to a specific career path (Selingo, 2013). However, environments that use a liberal arts curriculum can nurture students' curiosity for learning and build a foundation of 21st-century skills that employers seek. Students are challenged to think critically, collaborate, communicate, and influence others through complex problems—skills that enhance employability and marketability in a quickly changing landscape (Kamenetz, 2015). When technology is introduced as a vehicle to solve today's problems, students can showcase their ability to take calculated risks, learn new skills, and influence their peers.

Yet, higher education struggles to explain technological skills in the context of the labor market because these competencies are not being measured by traditional standardized tests (Kamenetz, 2015). According to the National Association of Colleges and Employers (NACE, 2015), hiring managers seek candidates who are able to solve problems quickly and efficiently by using technological tools to enhance their work. Skills like communication, teamwork, and problem solving top the wish list – skills that cut across many areas of academic and cocurricular activities (NACE,

2015). Students who are given opportunities to showcase their academic curiosity and capacity for leadership may be more likely to become skilled users and early adopters of technology. Many higher education leaders assume students from younger generations are mastering technological skills on their own and that they are prepared to apply them in their first jobs. Although this may be true for some, educators have made sweeping generalizations about students' technological competencies.

In a 2014 Gallup poll, both industry leaders and higher education administrators were asked if college graduates were prepared for today's ever-changing workforce (Calderon & Sidhu, 2014). The results indicated a clear mismatch: only 11% of industry leaders thought college graduates were prepared for the workforce whereas 96% of higher education leaders insisted that they were. As this gap shows, practitioners will need to work closely with students, administrators, and employers to adopt a growth mindset in educational and workspaces (Dweck, 2006). Embracing students' curiosity is the key to preparing them for leadership and life success beyond the academy.

Mindset for Career Curiosity

A proposed *mindset for career curiosity* was created based on the idea that if individuals are curious and willing to learn, apply, and teach new concepts, they will remain successful in work and life as effective digital leaders. The mindset is divided into three phases: learning, doing, and teaching. The theoretical framework includes research from Dweck (2006), Kolb (1984), and Bandura (1986). Practitioners can use this research to connect the mindset to practice and apply it to help students embrace technology, adapt to new environments, and lead through change in their first jobs and beyond.

Change can be difficult for any individual as they experience it as well as when they lead others through it. When disruption occurs, it can be approached through a fixed or growth mindset. Workers who are skeptical or afraid to embrace new technologies as they emerge may be demonstrating what Dweck (2012) refers to as a "fixed mindset". Those who are not open to change will become complacent in that particular environment. However, if employees are open to learning new skills, working hard to master them, and teaching them to others, higher education and workplaces will thrive. According to Dweck, individuals who demonstrate a growth mindset take on challenges with the understanding that skills can be developed through hard work and determination. In this instance, as new technology emerges, individuals with a growth mindset are drawn to the challenge of learning how to use new tools to become more productive through leading and engaging differently in the work culture. In order to meet the demands of 21st-century employers, educators and administrators will need to be nimble and responsive like in some entrepreneurial environments outside of academe.

NEW DIRECTIONS FOR STUDENT LEADERSHIP • DOI: 10.1002/yd

To complement the idea of growth mindsets in the context of career development, Kolb's (1984) model of experiential learning is often cited as the premise for college career settings, including internships, service learning, job shadowing, and other applied learning experiences. To add another layer to the mindset for career curiosity, Bandura's social cognitive theory (1986) introduces the idea of self-efficacy, or in this context, students being able to control their actions and successfully navigating digital spaces. Individuals are more likely to take risks if they believe they can succeed in a disrupted environment (Bandura, 1986). These career theories blended with an adapted growth mindset can help students, educators, and employees adapt and connect quickly to frequent changes in technology and society.

The mindset for career curiosity is designed to be used at any level of personal or professional engagement. It is applicable as early as middle school, as students register for personal email and social networking accounts, but it can also be used as a framework for middle-aged workers—any time individuals are ready to be more fully engaged in expanding their own development and digital identity. The mindset for career curiosity is built on a three-part framework of learning, doing, and teaching; where students can explore, apply, and then assist others in the acquisition of leadership skills, career knowledge, or life skills.

Individuals who have embraced the mindset for career curiosity can be at varying levels of technological leadership. Students and instructors embrace curiosity in their classrooms, in student activities and organizations, among communities they serve, abroad, through research, and in their workplace through jobs and internships. Students, educators, and employees who adopt this mindset to overcome technological challenges will begin to embody the skills employers seek: leadership, critical thinking, and teamwork. They may even have the ability to motivate and lead individuals who fear change and become complacent in their environments.

Phase I: Learning.   The first phase in this proposed mindset is *learning*, in which students demonstrate technological curiosity, make connections with expert users, and develop confidence to try new skills in applying technology to their leadership practices. At a basic level, graduates who are successful with navigating change must demonstrate the desire to learn new skills by experimenting with technology, even if success is not guaranteed. Curiosity is sometimes fueled by trial and error and through experiential learning, students will begin to see the benefits and pitfalls of learning and doing business in digital spaces.

When Facebook emerged on college campuses in 2004, students became early adopters of social media (GCN, 2007). Perhaps students were drawn to the prestige of using a Harvard-created social network or perhaps it was their existing level of comfort using technology. This cohort of students was one of the first to enter academia with technology tools like email, online course registration, and Google as a search engine (GCN, 2007). Although other social networks like Myspace and Friendster had been around for a few years, there were very few campus experts who could warn early adopters about social media's pitfalls. A base knowledge of technology, the desire to learn more, and the willingness to take risks played a pivotal role in shaping the way students approach emerging technology.

As students dive deeper into technology experimentation and as campuses begin to catch up, practitioners can be more proactive when addressing the challenges of a connected life. For example, whereas keyboarding used to be a standard part of the K–12 curriculum, topics like Internet safety, privacy and security, and cyberbullying are overarching themes that are a focus today. Now, instead of teaching students hard technical skills, instructors have begun offering lessons in critical thinking when it comes to online privacy, discretion, and informed decision making as students explore new tools and platforms. To assist, some campuses have incorporated digital identity components into orientation programs and first-year courses. Taking stock of students' online identities allows them to reflect on their digital footprints as they begin new chapters in their preprofessional lives. For example, at the State University of New York (SUNY) College at Oswego, the Career Services office runs an online auditing program for high school and college students called "Digital Dirt" (Qualman, 2015). During peer consultations, Digital Dirt Squad members comb through Google search results, tweets, Facebook posts, Instagram pictures, and other pieces of information that are permanently etched in cyberspace. After helping students see the trail of information they have left online, educators make sure students know their rights as online users and about strategies to keep their information appropriate, safe, and private.

As students begin building personal learning networks and modeling their online behaviors as more fluent technology users, another way to embrace the mindset is through connection. Once high school students have taken stock of their digital footprints and learned about their privacy rights, many begin using social media and other tools to make friends and build relationships. According to the Pew Research Center (2013), social media users have more close ties than nonusers, so it is recommended that higher education professionals maximize the digital space as a forum for building connections, tackling difficult issues, as well as celebrating career and personal leadership successes. The ability to easily forge close relationships, build trust, and influence others will help to groom the next generation of leaders.

Many campuses are leveraging various tools and platforms to help students to connect with their universities before their first day of classes. At George Mason University, customized connectors help students to build stronger contacts with employers, alumni, and faculty. These new relationship-based services transform students into hubs of connectivity (Dey & Cruzvergara, 2014b) designed to provide tailored advice, strategies, and feedback to constituents. As students move through their college careers, social media can help students to feel connected to their home communities (Ahlquist, 2014). National organizations use social media to engage emerging student leaders in common causes, including the White House #ItsOnUs campaign to end campus sexual violence and the American Association of University Women's #ElectHer program to encourage women student leaders to run for office. Similarly, national fraternities, sororities, and organizations like the NAACP have student and local campus chapters that use social media to educate, convene, and connect.

Similarly, as community and belonging are essential for students beginning to develop their personal brands, The George Washington University (GW) have created a life cycle Career Success Plan. GW's model, which spans 4 years, begins at orientation and culminates in a senior year FutureU series (Dunkins, 2014). Elements of FutureU were designed to connect students embarking on career exploration to student leaders who have similar goals. The overarching GW Career Success Plan is built on various pillars, including developing leadership skills, creating an online presence, exploring careers, industries and networks, and developing workplace skills. Throughout these experiences, student employees and student leaders are taught how to create a strong personal narrative and individual brand recognition. Likewise, as younger generations begin using social tools as an extension of their daily communication, many employers have also started leveraging social media from the recruitment side to connect and build goodwill with potential candidates.

A key method to using this framework is to build an online presence, develop confidence, and demonstrate comfort with experimentation. For example, students who create LinkedIn profiles are showcasing a positive online identity, demonstrating confidence by reaching out to new online connections, and broadening their professional networks. If higher education practitioners work to build stronger connections between first-year programs, career services, and digital identity initiatives, students will gain exposure to these types of online connection tools early in their college careers (Stoller, 2012). Building a stronger presence through social media will change the landscape for students and practitioners by helping students to make meaningful connections to their future professions. As career services practitioners Dey and Cruzvegara (2014b) noted, social media play a critical role when trying to establish a professional image that exudes credibility and likeability. As Dey and Cruzvergara (2014a) suggest in *10 Future Trends in Career Services*, emerging career development offices should focus on building connections and communities that foster a stronger network designed to promote student success.

Phase II: Doing.   The second phase in the mindset is *doing*, in which students begin to curate content and create their own. By curating, students can design, capture, and demonstrate materials they have pulled together, sifted through, and selected as elements for broader presentation. Stephen Bell (2016) wrote about the skills students need to be more effective lifelong learners, including accumulating and reporting their experiences. Bell's position is that there is a need for practical learning opportunities that complement the curriculum or help students become better problem solvers. Bell describes a progressive learning system that helps students to develop many different skills employers seek, while becoming lifelong learners.

Likewise, Pittinsky and Butty (2015) suggest a college's ability to create learning experiences is critical but higher education will need to move away from traditional models. Their position is that in order to be responsive to students, campuses will need to create clear paths for students with work experience, organizational leadership experience, and job skills. This will help guide students who expect custom experiences and programs that help them reach their career goals.

Employers who partner with academe can help support, develop, and demonstrate learning through projects that reflect leadership and other real world competencies. In the world of education today, employers care more about skills, the value of degrees, and the ability to connect disparate areas of knowledge and disciplines (Pittinsky & Butty, 2015). In their view, universities that thrive in this new era will embrace their role by curating educational experiences aligned with demands of the workforce. Thus, content can be gathered from individuals, groups, communities, courses, or crowdsourcing, allowing participants to upload, describe, and distribute this content in a widely useful and accessible manner that further connects students to their own learning, growth, and leadership development.

For students to actually implement the mindset, they must be able to create content and display it. In this way, students demonstrate their ability to do the work as they move from building on others' ideas to building their own. For example, a student might build a personal website that showcases their professional leadership portfolio and resume, create a newsletter from community service-learning experiences, submit an undergraduate research article for review, present at a conference, share artifacts from a student organization, or publish a blog. Displaying one's work publicly demonstrates a certain level of risk taking and vulnerability. According to a Pew Internet study (2013), 46% of social media users create original online content as opposed to 41% of users who only curate content. Some campuses are playing an integral role in supporting students in creating and presenting their content.

In *How Do I Assign and Assess 21st Century Work?* Fisher (2013) advocates for the use of the portfolio as a tool where students select their best work that represents proficiency over a period of time, include reflective statements, and articulate how it demonstrates student learning.

At the University of Mary Washington, the "Domain of One's Own" program allows every student to register a domain hosted on the university's web space. This immediately removes barriers for students and helps them begin establishing themselves as experts in their respective fields of study by sharing online. Faculty are able to teach lessons tied to various industry and academic areas while using technology to help students to reflect, build, and demonstrate competency through personal branding activities of students' current and future leadership experiences and academic endeavors.

Phase III: Teaching.   The third phase in the mindset is *teaching*, where students demonstrate competence with new technology tools by teaching others how to use them. At this point, competent individuals are able to demonstrate ways to use technology in productive, positive, and measurable ways with and for others. By teaching students to set personal and professional goals for technology use, it can influence career behaviors in very important ways. For example, if a high school student who participated in SUNY Oswego's Digital Dirt program was demonstrating competence, he or she might join the Digital Dirt Squad and become a peer support to younger students as a leader and role model.

Technology competency is often self-taught and gains tremendous force as students not only learn and do but also apply their knowledge by teaching or mentoring. Essentially, there are two types of workers in the digital space: those who do not *do* technology and those who take steps to figure out what is new and how it might be useful for themselves and others. For example, many campuses have seen increased demands of support for an incubator culture among students and student leaders, both in more corporate and business spheres as well as in social enterprise (Pappano, 2012). This small start-up sector has emerged on campuses, supported by student innovation and institutional infrastructure. At GW, that has sparked the creation of several new student-developed mobile apps and platforms, including one called *We Take Two* (Zauzmer, 2015). The app demonstrates students' computer science knowledge in action and applies it to serving others. Such examples (Pappano, 2012) represent trends seen in the past 5 years, as more and more schools are creating venues for this type of activity on campuses nationwide.

In the same vein, traditional job interviews are becoming a concept of the past, and candidates are being asked to show their work instead of just talking about it. As a result, hacking events have become increasingly popular, where developers, designers, and project managers develop and code software programs in real time, blending the student talent pipeline with that of more seasoned developers. Companies like AT&T have realized the value of events like these and have sponsored their own hackathon events to find talented candidates at all levels. According to AT&T (2016), innovation happens when you bring people together to collaborate on creative projects. Collaborative spaces, in person and online, can be used to help students and candidates to confidently demonstrate their skills and abilities to work in a team structure. Students often do this work through student or Greek life organizations, both as members and through e-board leadership, which we know are skills employers seek in college graduates (NACE, 2015). Accordingly, schools have embraced hacking cultures that extend beyond the curriculum, connections, and prestige of programs like those at Stanford and MIT (Pappano, 2012). Events like these encourage participants to demonstrate their skills in specific competency areas while interdependently learning from others in a collaborative exchange of information and ideas.

Mindset Application vs. Complacency. As technology continues to change rapidly, workers need to become lifelong learners, or they risk falling into a complacent, fixed mindset (Dweck, 2012). Once competency is reached in a certain skill area, students and workers have two choices: to complete work the way it has always been done or to find ways to stay ahead of the curve.

Bandura's social-cognitive theory (1986) indicates that self-efficacy allows individuals to exercise control over their actions and environment. Students or workers who have a growth mindset demonstrate risk taking and continuous strides toward mastery. Flexibility in the workplace demonstrates that they can use curiosity and problem-solving skills to approach challenges and shows consistent and sustained effort in solving new problems with technology. For example, as more learning happens in digital spaces, higher education has a choice to embrace new collaborative, online learning methods or to cling to traditional methods of instruction.

AirBnB is an example of how traditional workspaces have been transformed and how online and mobile technology have been used to lead new, successful business ideas while keeping overhead costs low and flexibility high. AirBnB, a website where people can list, find, and rent lodging, is the fifth largest national hospitality chain, despite having no property assets (Thomas, 2014). As technology is used to solve both simple and complex problems, educators will need to provide spaces for students to become pioneers in these new digital spaces.

Future Trends, Recommendations, and Predictions

In order to remain relevant in higher education, professionals should embrace a growth mindset, which encourages them to be nimble to meet the rapidly changing needs of the students they teach and the workforce students enter. This philosophy affects student and parent expectations around affordability, employer expectations of outcomes, our institutional responses, and environmental and organizational structures, as well as our pedagogical approaches to education. The ability to meet these challenges will likely require institutional commitment and a regular focus on the future.

External sources, including parents and employers, federal and state authorities, and accrediting bodies, argue about making higher education more measurable. Brown (2013) focuses on student learning in a digital age to include not only the acquisition of knowledge but also its application. Employers argue there is real value in having industry leaders using their external expertise to shape how higher education practitioners prepare students to graduate into a more diverse, nontraditional workforce, which is highly digital and multigenerational. That external pressure can serve to support, monitor, and ensure accountability on academic outcomes, which students, parents, and employers find appealing. At the price point of higher education today, the return on investment of having real-world skills like leadership, communication, problem solving, and teamwork (NACE, 2015) has become an expectation.

To adapt, higher education must change its organizational approach and structure to be successful in this climate. Many campuses are making growth orientation a priority, particularly through enhanced services and support around campus career development in higher education. In fact, Dey and Cruzvegara (2014b) noted leaders in higher education recognize the direct link career services have to recruitment, retention, and revenue. Institutions like GW, Wake Forest, and Wellesley are elevating career services (Dey & Cruzvegara, 2014a), giving their leaders more influence and the ability to convene internal and external stakeholders in order to help students leverage the broad power of university networks.

Additionally, as we think about the way the world has become hyperconnected, higher education practitioners and their students must continue to adapt quickly to a changing environmental landscape that has gone virtual, global, and mobile (Friedman & Mandelbaum, 2011). The traditional workplace can be defined as the *physical* space in which a person works. In the context of today's work environments, that definition must also include virtual spaces. With video conferencing, cloud computing, and mobile devices, employees can be productive anytime, anywhere, and with people all over the world. Digital work environments are not bound by space or physical boundaries, but they use technology to enhance collaboration, cost effectiveness, and ingenuity. Technology continues to remove barriers to productivity in classrooms and workplaces, but the rapid changes in these advances have also presented challenges for leaders. Thinking ahead, we must prepare students to work in rapidly changing environments and industries that do not yet exist.

To remedy this, schools must continue to innovate in their instructional delivery. Regarding pedagogy, the dynamic nature of online education is quickly changing the landscape of our most basic academic instruction and how, when, and where educational content is actually delivered. This is forcing some of the most dramatic change, evolution, and disruption in higher education—through external organizations like 2U, Coursera, and EdX, and as institutional leaders feel the pressure to maximize emerging online tools, develop massive online open courses (MOOCS), and create effective online course platforms. Going forward, there cannot be an option for faculty and other educators to opt out of using the digital space for instruction, reflection, and learning.

To keep pace, leaders in higher education have tried to connect with forward-thinking associations and those developing new professional standards, knowledge communities, and expanded online learning and teaching platforms. This has led to new technology competencies in leadership education (Ahlquist, 2014; Brown, 2013) that may soon become the norm in our professional development, credentialing, and training curriculum.

Conclusion

Organizations that wish to stay on the cutting edge of innovation must adopt a future-focused mindset for curiosity. The new normal embraces environments that encourage risk taking and are nimble, fast paced, and technologically savvy. Higher education must remain open to change as it finds new ways to engage students, parents, employers, and alumni.

References

Ahlquist, J. (2014). Trending now: Digital leadership education using social media and the social change model. *Journal of Leadership Studies*, 8(1), 57–60.

Anderson, M. (2015, April 9). Teens, social media & technology overview 2015. *Pew Research Center*. Retrieved from http://www.pewresearch.org/data-trend/media-and-technology/device-ownership/

AT&T Developer Program. (2016). AT&T mobile app hackathon. Retrieved from http://developer.att.com/events

Bandura, A. (1986). *Social foundations of thought and action: A social cognitive theory.* Upper Saddle River, NY: Prentice-Hall.

Bell, S. (2016, January 20). New opportunities in learning experienced curation: From the Bell tower. Retrieved from http://lj.libraryjournal.com/2016/01/opinion/steven-bell/new-opportunities-in-learning-experience-curation-from-the-bell-tower/#_

Brown, P. G. (2013). Re-envisioning student learning in a digital age. *About Campus*, 4(18), 30–32.

Calderon, V. J., & Sidhu, P. (2014). Business leaders say knowledge trumps college pedigree. *Gallup*. Retrieved from http://www.gallup.com/poll/167546/business-leaders-say-knowledge-trumps-college-pedigree.aspx

Carnevale, A., & Rose, J. (2015). *The economy goes to college: The hidden promise of higher education in the post industrial service economy.* Washington, DC: Georgetown Center on Education and the Workforce, Georgetown University.

Dey, F., & Cruzvergara, C. Y. (2014a). 10 future trends in college career services. *LinkedIn*. Retrieved from https://www.linkedin.com/pulse/20140715120812-11822737-10-future-trends-in-college-career-services

Dey, F., & Cruzvergara, C. (2014b). Evolution of career services in higher education. In K. K. Smith (Ed.), *New Directions for Student Services: No. 148. Strategic directions for career services within the university setting* (pp. 5–18). San Francisco, CA: Jossey-Bass.

Dunkins, B. (2014, February 5). FutureU teaches life lessons 101. *GW Today*. Retrieved from https://gwtoday.gwu.edu/futureu-teaches-life-lessons-101

Dweck, C. (2006). *Mindset: The new psychology of success.* New York, NY: Ballantine Books.

Dweck, C. (2012). *Mindset: How you can fulfill your potential.* New York, NY: Ballantine Books.

Fisher, M. (2013). *Digital learning strategies: How do I assign and assess 21st century work?* Alexandria, VA: Association for Supervision and Curriculum Development.

Friedman, T. L., & Mandelbaum, M. (2011). *That used to be us: How America fell behind in the world it invented and how we can come back.* New York, NY: Farrar, Straus, and Giroux.

Fry, R. (2015, May 11). Millennials surpass Gen Xers as the largest generation in U.S. labor force. *Pew Research Center*. Retrieved from http://www.pewresearch.org/fact-tank/2015/05/11/millennials-surpass-gen-xers-as-the-largest-generation-in-u-s-labor-force/

GCN. (2007, December 6). 25 years: A technology timeline. *GCN Magazine*. Retrieved from https://gcn.com/Articles/2007/12/06/25-years-A-technology-timeline.aspx

Kamenetz, A. (2015, May 28). Nonacademic skills are key to success. But what should we call them? Retrieved from http://www.npr.org/sections/ed/2015/05/28/404684712/non-academic-skills-are-key-to-success-but-what-should-we-call-them

Kolb, D. A. (1984). *Experiential learning: Experience as the source of learning and development*. Englewood Cliffs, NJ: Prentice Hall.

Lenhart, A. (2015, April 9). Teens, social media & technology overview 2015. *Pew Research Center*. Retrieved from http://www.pewinternet.org/2015/04/09/teens-social-media-technology-2015/

National Association of Colleges and Employers. (2015, November 18). Job outlook 2016. Retrieved from http://www.naceweb.org/s11182015/employers-look-for-in-new-hires.aspx

Pappano, L. (2012, July 20). Got the next great idea? *New York Times*. Retrieved from http://www.nytimes.com/2012/07/20/education/edlife/campus-incubators-are-on-the-rise-as-colleges-encourage-student-start-ups.html?_r=0

Pew Research Center. (2013, December 7). Social networking fact sheet. Retrieved from http://www.pewinternet.org/fact-sheets/social-networking-fact-sheet/

Pittinsky, M., & Butty, M. (2015, December 30). The new college degree: In an unbundled world, curation is king. *Edsurge*. Retrieved from https://www.edsurge.com/news/2015-12-30-the-new-college-degree-in-an-unbundled-word-curation-is-king

Qualman, E. (2015). *What happens on campus stays on YouTube*. Cambridge, MA: Equalman Studios.

Selingo, J. J. (2013). *College (un)bound: The future of higher education and what it means for Students*. Las Vegas, NV: Amazon Publishing.

Stoller, E. (2012, February 8). Digital identity development: Orientation and career services. *Inside Higher Ed*. Retrieved from https://www.insidehighered.com/blogs/digital-identity-development-orientation-and-career-services

Thomas, P. (2014). Disrupt or be disrupted—it is inevitable. The disruptive workplace is here. *LinkedIn*. Retrieved from https://www.linkedin.com/pulse/20140723010242-1127749-disrupt-or-be-disrupted-it-is-inevitable-the-disruptive-workplace-is-here

Zauzmer, J. (2015, February 9). Three GW roommates are selling ads to give money away—maybe to you. *Washington Post*. Retrieved from https://www.washingtonpost.com/local/education/three-gw-roommates-want-to-give-money-to-charity-and-maybe-to-you/2016/02/09/9875a6fa-cebd-11e5-b2bc-988409ee911b_story.html

NEW DIRECTIONS FOR STUDENT LEADERSHIP • DOI: 10.1002/yd

MALLORY BOWER is the associate director of career services and strategic communication professor at the State University of New York (SUNY) College at Oswego. During her 10 years working in higher education, she has served on the SUNY Career Development Organization Board and the ACPA Commission for Career Development Directorate. She has helped hundreds of student leaders articulate their strengths through her work with the National Association for Campus Activities and the Association of College Unions International.

PETER KONWERSKI is the vice provost and dean of student affairs at the George Washington University. In addition to managing a nimble student affairs division, he strives to be a connected digital leader, working to support student success and develop our next generation of citizen leaders.

NEW DIRECTIONS FOR STUDENT LEADERSHIP • DOI: 10.1002/yd

Index

About.Me, 41
Abstract conceptualization (AC), 55
Active experimentation (AE), 55
Ahlquist, J., 6, 8, 9, 10, 11, 18, 35, 41,
    42, 47, 51, 56, 57, 62, 94, 99
AirBnB, 97
Alavi, M., 75
Alge, B. J., 84
Allen, S., 49
Allen, S. J., 80
American Institute of Parliamentarians,
    29
Americans' Internet Access, 49
Amichai-Hamburger, Y., 27, 30
Andenoro, A. C., 80
Anderson, J., 38
Anderson, M., 90
AOL Instant Messenger, 25
Argyris, C., 24

Bailey, G. D., 56
Balch, T. J., 29
Bandura, A., 28, 91, 92
Barr, M. J., 16
Bass, B. M., 49
Baumgartner, L. M., 23, 25
Bearden, S., 35, 38, 42, 44
Bell, S., 94
Bess, J. L., 17
Bill 78, 67
Billing, T. K., 77
Bishop, S. C., 12
Blab, 37
Black Lives Matter (BLM), 64, 67–69
Blaschke, L. M., 23, 25, 28
Blascovich, J., 76
Blessinger, P., 15
Blimling, G. S., 16
Bohmer, R. M., 82
Bono, J. E., 77
Bowen, W. G., 11, 12
Bower, M., 89, 101
boyd, d., 39, 48
boyd, d. m., 14

boyd, s., 47, 48
Bronfenbrenner, U., 22
Brooks, D. C., 13, 16
Brown, M. G., 12
Brown, P. G., 9, 10, 11, 20, 57, 97, 99
Burns, M. A., 64, 70
Butty, M., 95
Buvat, J., 10

Cabellon, E. T., 9, 14, 15, 16, 20
Caffarella, R. S., 23, 25
Calderon, V. J., 91
Caren, N., 66
Carnevale, A., 90
Castells, M., 83
Chait, J., 39
Chen, B., 49
Chen, P. D., 12
Chi, B., 36, 41, 42
Citizenship, defined, 35
Collins, M., 23
Common Core State Standards
    (CCSS), 23
Competency and capability, distinction
    between, 25. *See also* Leadership
    2.0
Concrete experience (CE), 55
Conner, J. M., 12
Cook, J. M., 84
Council for the Advancement of
    Standards in Higher Education, 77
Craig, S. B., 76
Cruzvergara, C., 93, 94, 98
Cruzvergara, C. Y., 94, 98
Curran, M. B. F. X., 35, 36, 39, 42, 43,
    44, 46

Dahlstrom, E., 13, 16
Dalton, J. C., 9
Dare, L. A., 15
Dee, C., 41
Dee, J. R., 17
Delzer, K., 40

Dennis, A. R., 85
Dey, F., 93, 94, 98
Digital Branding, 57–58
Digital citizenship, 11; defined, 36; elements, 37
Digital commerce, 39
Digital Community Building, 58. See also Digital student leadership development
Digital Dirt, 93
Digital etiquette, 37. See also P-20 digital citizenship model
Digital health and wellness, 39
Digital identity, 56
Digital law, 38
Digital leadership education pillars, 54
Digital literacy, 38
Digital security, 39
Digital student leadership development, 47–48; college student leader digital experience, 50–51; digital age, leadership in, 49–50; digital timeline, 51–54; future prospects, 59–61; pillars of, 54–59; students' attraction to social media, 48–49
Ditzler, C., 12
Donovan, J., 43, 44
Double-loop learning, 24
Douglas, T., 35, 36
Dowdy, L., 43, 44
Dugan, J. P., 25, 49, 50, 80
Duggan, M., 13, 15, 49
Dunkins, B., 94
Dunlap, J. C., 15
Dweck, C., 90, 91, 97

Easton, E. W., 14
Eaton, P., 10
Edmondson, A. C., 82
Eligon, J., 68
Ellison, N., 12, 49
Ellison, N. B., 14 15
Ellsworth, F. L., 64, 70
Endersby, L., 8, 75, 88
Evans, W. J., 29

Facebook, 14, 25
Face-to-face (F2F), 76
Fear of Missing Out (FOMO), 40

Fisher, M., 95
Fitzgerald, B., 22
Fixed mindset, 91. See also 21st-century workplace
Foldy, E., 25
Fox, S., 27, 30
Friedman, T. L., 98
Friendster, 92
Fry, R., 89
FutureU, 94

Gaby, S., 66
Garrison, M. J., 12
George Washington University (GW), 94
Getman, J., 11
Geys, B., 12
Gikas, J., 15
Gilster, P., 38
Ginwright, S. A., 68
Gismondi, A., 10, 17, 63, 65, 70, 74
Gitimu, P., 48
Goode, J., 22
Goodhue, D. L., 85
Google, 76
Google Hangout, 37
Grajek, S., 13, 16
Grant, M. M., 15
Grey, R., 14
Grinberg, E., 64
Guidry, K. R., 12

Haber-Curran, P., 49, 80
Harper, R., 14
Harper, S. R., 17
Hase, S., 23
Hassan, M., 12
Heiberger, G., 14
Help Desk, 41
Hernández, E., 63, 70, 71, 72
Heutagogy, 23
Hickey, D. T., 12
Higher Education Research Institute (HERI), 49
Hines, M. B., 12
Hoch, J. E., 27
Hoffman, J. L., 21, 33
Hogan, R., 76
Hollandsworth, R., 43, 44
Honemann, D. H., 29

Hong, E., 12
Hood, D. W., 48
Hoyt, C. L., 76
Huang, R., 76
Huang, W. H. D., 48

iCitizen Project, 42–43
Information and communication
    technologies (ICT), 78
Information technology (IT), 83
Instagram, 14, 25, 93
International Society for Technology in
    Education (ISTE), 10, 23

Järvelä, S., 15
Jaschik, S., 9
Jenkins, D., 75, 88
Jenkins, D. M., 79, 80
Jones, S. R., 17
Joosten, T., 14
Junco, R., 14, 47, 48, 56

Kahne, J., 36, 41, 42
Kaiser, R. B., 76
Kamenetz, A., 90
Kang, C., 37
Katz, E., 76
Kay, R. H., 11
Kennelly, J., 65, 67
Kenyon, C., 23
Khatib, N. M., 21
Khera, O., 11
Kim, M. K., 11
Kim, S. M., 11
Klein, H. J., 84
Kodama, C. M., 25
Kolb, D. A., 55, 91, 92
Kolomitz, K., 16
Komives, S. R., 27, 28, 49, 50
Konwerski, P., 89, 101
Kop, T., 22
Kottler, E., 21
Kozlowski, S. W., 27
Kuk, L., 15

Ladd, H. F., 22
Lahiri, S., 77
Lambert, A. D., 12
Lampe, C., 15, 49
LaRiviere, K., 50

Laru, J., 15
Lauricella, S., 11
Laurillard, D., 21
Lauzon, A. C., 23
Leadership 2.0, 21–22; leadership
    development practice, 28–31;
    leadership development theory,
    27–28; virtual and physical
    contexts, 22–27
Leadership education, technology in,
    9–10; digital tools, 13–15; impact
    of, 10–12; recommendations,
    15–17; student leaders and
    educators, 12–13
Leadership identity development
    (LID), 27
Leadership in the Digital Age, 59
Lederman, D., 9
Lenhart, A., 90
Lerman, K., 76
Lewis, P., 65, 66
Lieberman, D. A., 23
LinkedIn, 41, 94
Li, Y., 76
Logan, T. J., 14
Longerbeam, S. D., 27, 28
Lowenthal, P. R., 15
Lucas, N., 49
Luce, S., 65, 66
Luckin, R., 22
Luokkanen, T., 15

MacKenzie, D. A., 84
Mainella, F., 28
Mainella, F. C., 27, 28
Mandelbaum, M., 98
Maple Spring, 67
Marcus, J., 49
Martinez, E., 22
Martin, R., 27
Ma, S., 76
Massive online open courses
    (MOOCS), 98
Matias, A., 14
McClennan, G. S., 16
McCrea, B., 37
McMahon, T. R., 49
McPherson, M., 84
McWilliams, J., 12
Means, A. J., 12
Meltzoff, A. N., 40

Merriam, S. B., 23, 25
Middaugh, E., 36, 41, 42
Milkman, R., 65, 66
Morel, V., 10
Mukherjee, D., 77
Myspace, 25, 48, 92

Nadeau-Dubois, G., 67
National Association of Colleges and
    Employers (NACE), 90
National Association of
    Parliamentarians, 29
Näykki, P., 15
Networked publics, 48
New, J., 63, 64, 71

Occupy Wall Street, 64, 65–66
Ohler, J., 35
O'Meara, K., 50
Orlikowski, W., 80
Ospina, S., 25
Osteen, L., 27, 28, 63, 74, 80
Owen, J. E., 27, 28

Papert, S., 83
Pappano, L., 96
P–20 digital citizenship model, 35–36;
    community approach, 43–44;
    curriculum, 36–43; historical
    context, 36; recommendations for,
    44
Pearson, M., 68
Pérez-Peña, R., 68
Periscope, 37
Perrin, A., 13, 49
Pew Research Center, 89
Phelps, K., 75, 88
Pisano, G. P., 82
Pittinsky, M., 95
Prensky, M., 49
Project-based learning (PBL), 42
Purvanova, R. K., 77

Qualman, E., 11, 17, 57, 58, 93
Quebec Tuition Protests, 66–67

Raine, L., 38
Reeves, J., 13, 16
Reflective observation (RO), 55
Reimold, D., 66

Rettner, R., 40
Ribble, M., 5, 35, 36, 37, 38, 39, 40, 42,
    44, 46, 57
Ribble, M. S., 56
Riggio, R. E., 27
Robert, H. M., 29
Robert, S. C., 29
Roberts-Mahoney, H., 12
Robert's Rules of Order, 29
Rogers, E. M., 84
Rosas, M., 64
Rose, J., 90
Rosen, S., 21, 22
Ross, D., 77
Rossman, M. H., 23
Ross, T. W., 56

Sandeen, A., 16
Scheffer, J., 41, 44
Schön, D., 24
Schradie, J., 64
Schuh, J. H., 17
Seaton, W. J., 23
Selingo, J. J., 90
Selwyn, N., 25
Senge, P. M., 24
Serven, R., 68
Shand, K., 21
Shankman, M., 49
Shirky, C., 17
Sidhu, P., 91
Skype, 37, 58
Slack, 80
Smith, A., 72
Smith, C., 67
Smith-Lovin, L., 84
Snapchat, 25
Snider, J., 50
Social media, 12, 23, 41, 64
Social technologies and leadership
    education, 13–14
Somashekhar, S., 65, 69
Sowcik, M., 80
Spitzer, B., 10
Sponcil, M., 48
Spriggs, D., 22
Stackpole, J. D., 29
State University of New York (SUNY),
    58, 93
21st-century workplace: career
    curiosity, 91–97; characteristics of,

89–90; college graduates,
employers seek in, 90–91; future
prospects, 97–99
Steinfield, C., 15, 49
Stoller, E., 94
Stromberg, A., 50
Strudler, N., 12
Subrahmanyam, K. V. J., 10
Sullivan, T., 41
Surfacing mental models, 24
Sylvester, N., 29

Tashakkori, A., 50
Technocentrism, 83
*Technology Addiction: Concern,
Controversy and Finding Balance*, 35
Technology age, student activism in,
63–64; case studies, 65–69;
digitally aided movements, 64–65;
implications for practice, 70–72;
lessons learned, 69–70
Teddlie, C., 50
Thomas, A. G., 15
Thomas, G., 27
Thomas, P., 90, 97
Thompson, R. L., 85
Toffler, A., 38
Toyoma, K., 84
Trello, 78
Tripp, N., 43
Tufekci, Z., 65
Tumblr, 66
Twitter, 12, 14

Valacich, J. S., 85
Vigdor, J. L., 22
Virtual table and digital technology,
75–76, 85–87; standards and
competencies for virtual

leadership, 77; team virtuality,
77–78; virtual leadership
competency, 80–85; virtual
leadership considerations, 76–77,
78–80
Vitak, J., 14
Von Krogh, G., 77
Vorhies, C., 21, 33

Wainapel, G., 27, 30
Wajcman, J., 84
Wallace, J., 42
Walton, P., 22
Wankel, C., 15
We Are the 99 Percent, 66
WeChat, 25
Wiethoff, C., 84
Wikipedia, 76
Wilson, C., 65
Winstead, L., 21
Wohn, D. Y., 12
Wolf, D. F., 14
Wolfe, T. M., 68
Wong, A., 63, 72
Wu, X., 76
Wyatt, N., 67

Yan, X., 76
Yik Yak, 25
Yoo, S. J., 48
Yoo, Y., 75
YouTube, 29, 48

Zapata, L. P., 15
Zauzmer, J., 96
Zhang, Y., 76
Zoom, 58
Zuboff, S., 83

NEW DIRECTIONS FOR STUDENT LEADERSHIP

ORDER FORM SUBSCRIPTION AND SINGLE ISSUES

DISCOUNTED BACK ISSUES:

Use this form to receive 20% off all back issues of *New Directions for Student Leadership*.
All single issues priced at **$23.20** (normally $29.00)

TITLE	ISSUE NO.	ISBN

Call 1-800-835-6770 or see mailing instructions below. When calling, mention the promotional code JBNND to receive your discount. For a complete list of issues, please visit www.wiley.com/WileyCDA/WileyTitle/productCd-YD.html

SUBSCRIPTIONS: (1 YEAR, 4 ISSUES)

☐ New Order ☐ Renewal

U.S.	☐ Individual: $89	☐ Institutional: $363
CANADA/MEXICO	☐ Individual: $89	☐ Institutional: $405
ALL OTHERS	☐ Individual: $113	☐ Institutional: $441

Call 1-800-835-6770 or see mailing and pricing instructions below.
Online subscriptions are available at www.onlinelibrary.wiley.com

ORDER TOTALS:

Issue / Subscription Amount: $ _____

Shipping Amount: $ _____
(for single issues only – subscription prices include shipping)

Total Amount: $ _____

SHIPPING CHARGES:

First Item	$6.00
Each Add'l Item	$2.00

(No sales tax for U.S. subscriptions. Canadian residents, add GST for subscription orders. Individual rate subscriptions must be paid by personal check or credit card. Individual rate subscriptions may not be resold as library copies.)

BILLING & SHIPPING INFORMATION:

☐ **PAYMENT ENCLOSED:** *(U.S. check or money order only. All payments must be in U.S. dollars.)*

☐ **CREDIT CARD:** ☐ VISA ☐ MC ☐ AMEX

Card number _____ Exp. Date _____

Card Holder Name _____ Card Issue # _____

Signature _____ Day Phone _____

☐ **BILL ME:** *(U.S. institutional orders only. Purchase order required.)*

Purchase order # _____
Federal Tax ID 13559302 • GST 89102-8052

Name _____

Address _____

Phone _____ E-mail _____

Copy or detach page and send to: **John Wiley & Sons, Inc. / Jossey Bass**
PO Box 55381
Boston, MA 02205-9850

PROMO JBNND

CPSIA information can be obtained
at www.ICGtesting.com
Printed in the USA
BVOW09s0734151117
500331BV00016B/186/P

9 781119 378556